Quest for Middle-earth

Quest for Middle-earth

Dirk Vander Ploeg

iUniverse, Inc.
New York Lincoln Shanghai

Quest for Middle-earth

iUniverse books may be ordered through booksellers or by contacting:

iUniverse
2021 Pine Lake Road, Suite 100
Lincoln, NE 68512
www.iuniverse.com
1-800-Authors (1-800-288-4677)

The views expressed in this work are solely those of the author and do not necessarily reflect the views of the publisher, and the publisher hereby disclaims any responsibility for them.

ISBN: 978-0-595-44093-1 (pbk)
ISBN: 978-0-595-88417-9 (ebk)

Printed in the United States of America

Contents

Introduction

The pursuit of truth is the genesis of the quest!

J.R.R. Tolkien in his tale *The Lord of the Rings* presents to us a landscape populated by people that are very similar to what we recognize as our 'real world.' Indeed the interactions of his characters remind us of ourselves and others we know.

While reading his epic and then witnessing Peter Jackson's movie adaptation I wondered what was Tolkien's inspiration for his stories. Both the book and movie mention that "The Dominion of Men" had arrived. I could not shake the idea that if "The Dominion of Men" had arrived, what had existed before it?

Tolkien was an Oxford University professor of Anglo-Saxon and English language. As such he was captivated by myths from the North countries and actually learned Finnish so that he could read the ancient tales in their original language. He was particularly mesmerized by a collection of ruins, known as the *Kalevala*, which has been compared to Homer's *Odyssey*. He also knew the myths of the Norse God Odin, king of the Vikings and owner of a ring that bound other rings and their wearers to him. Other tales that he studied included *The Saga of the Ring* and *The Kingdom of the Circle*.

He believed that myths and fairy stories were means of conveying certain transcendent truths to Man. "I believe that legends and myths are largely made of "truth", and indeed present aspects of it that can only be received in this mode; and long ago certain truths and modes were discovered and must always reappear."

The *Bible* and the *Book of Enoch* tell of a group of angels that descended from heaven and took women as their wives. They bore children that were taller, stronger and more intelligent than normal. These children were the demigods (half mortal and half god) of historical Characters with names like Achilles, Apollo, Hercules, Jason and Thor became the heroes of our myths and legends and superheroes of their own movies, television series, cartoons and comic books.

There is evidence that The Lord of the Rings was based on actual historical events! New archeological evidence from Sumer, Babylon, Greece and Finland suggest that intelligent creatures once lived and worked harmoniously with Mankind. Clues point to the fact that as a race, we were the labor force required to serve superior beings—gods—to create their vision of heaven on earth.

This is an excellent hypothesis but can any of it be proven. Are there answers to my questions? My quest for Middle-earth begins.

BOOK ONE

1

Erich von Daniken's Chichén Itzá

The twin prop, which held about twenty passengers and crew, landed on the dirt runway sometime after daybreak. It was 1977 and this was the first trip out of the country that my wife Sally and I had taken. We had left the beautiful resort island of Cozumel about an hour earlier. I'd had to literally beg her to take this expensive side trip. She momentarily abandoned her fear of motion sickness and reluctantly agreed.

So here we were bouncing down a runway that was really just a patch of dirt hewn out of the living jungle. Fog was drifting alongside our aircraft obscuring our initial view of this unknown country. You had to hand it to the Mexicans: this runway was a monument to their entrepreneurial spirit. Without it, vacationers would have to travel by bus or car to reach this isolated area. Now tourists had the opportunity to see and experience ancient history firsthand.

After exiting the plane we followed a tour guide through the jungle toward the ruins. We were standing in a cleared field and stretching before us were ancient structures that had been literally dug and cut out of the jungle. Thick trees and bushes were beaten back and mounds of earth removed, providing breathing space for a city some say was over 1,500 years old.

Towering before us and reaching up toward heaven was a great pyramid. We stared in awe. We exchanged 'do you believe this?' nods and approached the pyramid eagerly. We chose the closest stairway and were greeted by two colossal serpent heads with gaping mouths and protruding tongues. These sculpted heads were the guardians of the stairways. During the equinox, the combination of sun and shade create the illusion that each serpent's body is moving down the pyramid.

We started our ascent. Mayan pyramids consist of nine levels or tiers, decreasing in size as the structure goes higher. Each of the four sides of the pyramid have a stairway consisting of exactly ninety-one steps and counting the top platform they make up a total of 365 representing the number of days in a calendar year.

I was a bit exhausted after arriving at the top. This platform atop the structure housed a temple. The temple had four doorways, which faced the four directions of the compass. Its large chamber was amazingly cool under the morning sun. This pyramid and temple were known as 'El Castillo' or 'the castle.'

El Castillo also called the castle.

As we walked out of the temple, it took a few seconds for our eyes to adjust to the brightness of the morning light. Surveying the area we saw the crumbling buildings of the ancient city below. Beyond the buildings were trees and beyond the trees was a jungle. From this height the green and black canopy of overgrowth suffocated the city and one had to wonder how long it would take for the jungle to reclaim it.

There was no wind—only heat. The sun was low in the morning sky, but its pulsating rays had already burned away the predawn fog. The grass surrounding the castle looked burnt and worn showing traces of the rich red earth beneath. We were standing atop the great pyramid at Chichén Itzá in Yucatan, Mexico.

From our vantage point we could easily see the Observatory, also known as the Carocal. It was almost directly south of El Castillo and looked like modern observatories everywhere. I half-expected to see a giant telescope protruding through the opening of the observatory's crumbling dome and ancient Mayans peering through the lens and dictating their findings to their apprentices. Turning away from the Observatory we walked back into the temple and imagined what horrors may have been committed there.

The Mayans practiced bloodletting, which was carried out to appease the gods, and when their civilization began to fall, rulers with large territories rushed from one city to the other, performing blood rites in order to maintain the status quo.

For the Maya, blood sacrifice was necessary for the survival of both gods and people, sending human energy skyward and receiving divine power in return. A king used an obsidian knife or a stingray spine to cut his penis, allowing the blood to fall onto paper held in a bowl. Kings' wives also took part in this ritual by pulling a rope with thorns attached through their tongues. The bloodstained paper was burned, the rising smoke directly communicating with the Sky World.

Human sacrifice was practiced on prisoners, slaves, and particularly children, with orphans and illegitimate children specially purchased for the occasion.

Recently, scientists working in Mexico have uncovered a lilac-colored stone knife and two skeletons, which they believe belonged to persons of Maya royal blood. One of the bodies was colored with vermilion, which is a bright red mercuric sulfide. Archaeologist Oscar Quintana asserts that what has been found is the previously undiscovered center of a Mayan blood cult. American anthropologist David Webster states that the Maya took almost sadistic pleasure in battles and fighting. Evidence has been found that indicates that the Maya used severed human heads as soccer balls in sporting events.

After descending the stairs we were led to a passageway hidden in the shadows of the pyramid. The castle is built upon an earlier pyramid, which is evident only when exploring the interior. This inside passage is not for the claustrophobic, and leads to an enclosed staircase that leads to the chac mul, an altar where sacrificial hearts were placed to be offered to the Gods.

Erich von Daniken initially introduced me to Chichén Itzá in his best selling book *Chariots of the Gods*.

The 1970 book not only tells a fabulous tale of extraterrestrial intelligent life visiting earth but also suggests that these visitors may have "produced a new, perhaps the first, Homo Sapiens." Von Daniken used extraordinary photographs from countries around the world, as evidence to prove his hypothesis. One of the photos permanently etched into my brain was of a Mayan observatory, a stone building created to study the heavens before the invention of the telescope.

Erich von Daniken was one of the first writers to ask the questions science didn't want to answer. Even today, thirty-five years later, scientists continue to parrot dogma taught to them in university. When was it that science and scientists forgot to ask the question, "What if …?"

As a direct result of the popularity of von Daniken and his controversial theories a 60-minute documentary movie was produced. The television special was entitled "In Search Of Ancient Astronauts," and was hosted and narrated by Rod

Serling, creator and host of the Twilight Zone. It aired in 1973 and was seen by thousands of curious viewers. I admit that I was one of those viewers and this broadcast convinced me that UFOs are real and that extraterrestrial life has indeed visited earth in our ancient past.

We continued our day at Chichén Itzá by visiting the Observatory, also known as the Carocal. Several of its windows point towards the equinox sunset and the southernmost and northernmost points on the horizon where Venus rises.

The Caracol or Observatory.

Next, we followed a well-worn path that led to the Sacred Cenote. A cenote is a sinkhole in a limestone bed, but it reminded us of a quarry. The cenote was the major source of water for the city dwellers. An underground river fed it. The sides of the cenote were sheer and it certainly didn't look very refreshing. In fact the water looked green and quite unappetizing.

The Ball court where players lost their heads.

We then also visited the Great Ball court, which has a playing area that is 545 feet long and 225 feet wide. The Mayans played a game that involved two teams and the players were only allowed to hit the ball with their elbows, wrists or hips. The object of the game was to knock the ball through one of the stone hoops on the walls of the court. The stone hoops were attached to the walls of the court and were twenty feet high.

Carvings on the lower walls of the court depict one team member with blood spurting out of his neck and another holding a decapitated head high. One can only assume that the headless man was the captain of the losing and not the winning team. It is said that a whisper from one end of the ball court can be heard clearly at the other end 500 feet away. The sound is seemingly unaffected by wind direction or time of day. No one has solved this riddle and it remains just one of many of the mysteries of Chichén Itzá!

Since visiting Chichén Itzá I have also explored the Mayan cities of Uxmal and Tulum. This was my first quest: the quest to find Erich von Daniken's Chichén Itzá.

In the late 1990s I had the opportunity to meet Erich von Daniken when he was in St. Catharines, Ontario, Canada. Mr. von Daniken was the head speaker at a paranormal related conference held there. Robert McConnell, host of the X-Zone Radio show, organized the event. One night after the conference we went out to dinner and I had the good fortune to be able to personally meet and speak with von Daniken. My wife, Carolyn Mahon, took the above photograph.

2

The Glorious Quest

The Lord of the Rings is ultimately a tale of quests. Frodo's quest is to return the One Ring to Mount Doom and to destroy the dark lord Sauron. The second quest is a romantic tale of forbidden love. It is the tale of Arwen, daughter of an Elf-Lord, who is forbidden to marry her childhood sweetheart, prince Aragorn. And the third quest involves healing the land of Gondor by returning its rightful king.

Frodo's quest is to return the One Ring to Mount Doom, from which it was forged, and then to throw it into the molten lava. But the dark lord is searching for the One Ring and has sent forth his spies and riders to seek Frodo out and to return the One Ring to him. Frodo is accompanied on his quest by his gardener Sam. Frodo is the knight errant and Sam his faithful squire. This partnership at times seems more reminiscent of Don Quixote and Sancho Panza than it is to Sir Lancelot and Kanahins.

Arwen and Aragorn's relationship, although an intricate part of the story is overshadowed by Frodo's quest and the War of the Ring. But it is in this relationship that we find two grail themes that are central to the story, and by their fulfillment fuse the tales together, creating not only a literary classic but reawakening the truth hidden in Grail and Ring mythology.

The Grail in this context doesn't refer to the cup Jesus drank from at the last supper, but rather to the interpretation found in ancient texts that refer to the Sang Real, or Royal Blood. The Ring has always been emblematic of kingship and is interchangeable with the Grail when referring to kingship and the royal blood.

Arwen, as Tolkien informs us was a princess of the Elven race. As such she was immortal and carried the matrilineal seed, the royal blood of the Elves. Aragorn was a prince and the rightful heir to Gondor. He carried the royal blood of kings. But he was mortal, and Arwen's father Elrond did not want his daughter to suffer when Aragorn died. So he forbade her to marry and planned for her to sail to the West.[1]

The second Grail theme mirrors the Arthurian legend. King Arthur is deceived into making love to his sister Morgana who becomes pregnant and delivers Arthur's child, Mordred. This act against God causes a cloud of despair to descend over Camelot, draining the king, people and crops of energy and sustenance. As his people starve, Arthur's health and hope fade. When all seems lost, Arthur sends his knights to find the Holy Grail and deliver it to him. Percival de Gales, one of King Arthur's knights, finally after many trials discovers the whereabouts of the Holy Grail but must first answer the question "Who does the grail serve?" Percival answers, "The Grail serves the King!" At which point the secret of the grail is revealed, the "land and the king are one." He returns with the grail cup from which Arthur drinks and he and the land are reborn.

Aragorn is faced with a similar dilemma. The White Tree of Gondor, the symbol of Gondor, is withering and dying as a result of Sauron's evil influence over Middle-earth. Likewise, the people of Gondor are suffering because a steward, having no king is ruling them. As Percival discovered in his grail quest, the land and king are one. As a result Gondor cannot be saved or reborn until it has a rightful king.

JRR Tolkien writes that: myth and fairy-story must, as all art, reflect and contain in solution elements of moral and religious truth (or error), but not explicit, not in the known form of the primary 'real' world.[2] In the first book of *The Lord of the Rings*, *The Fellowship of the Ring*, members of the fellowship first meet at the council of Elrond, in Rivendell. Elrond is their host and an Elven King. He summons the hobbits to him. He looked gravely at Frodo, "Do you still hold to your word, Frodo, that you will be the Ring-bearer?"[3]

"I do," said Frodo. "I will go with Sam."

Elrond stated that the number of the fellowship would total nine. Frodo and Sam and of course, Gandalf the Grey make up the first three. Then Elrond suggests, "For the rest, they shall represent the other Free Peoples of the World: Elves, Dwarves, and Men; Legolas shall be for the Elves; and Gimil son of Gloin for the Dwarves. They are willing to go at least to the passes of the Mountains, and maybe beyond. For men you shall have Aragorn son of Arathron, for the Ring of Isidur concerns him closely."[4]

The above paints a canvas for our imagination. Hobbits, Elves, Dwarves and Men, dressed in armor and chain mail, with helmets, knives, shields and swords at the ready, prepared for battle. The combination of JRR Tolkien's timeless literary classics and Peter Jackson's marvelously directed trilogy of The Lord of the

Rings is so realistic that one believes that he or she is actually a witness to history. Which begs the question: is there proof that Tolkien's inspiration for *The Lord of the Rings, The Hobbit* and *The Silmarillion*, were based on ancient myths and forgotten history?

Is there proof that man once shared this world with beings described as elves, dwarves or hobbits? What empirical evidence have archaeologists discovered if any?

Archaeologists have discovered various sites around the world that when excavated unearthed the preserved remains and personal artifacts of men that were at least six foot six inches tall and woman that were over six feet. These are believed to be the graves of Elves and Elf-lords. They had light brown to red hair, pale eyes, were leather clad and lived in a vast world that stretched from Transylvania to Tibet! History now teaches us that these were the ancestors of the Gaelic and Celtic High Kings who were among the most awesome warriors of all history.

Would you believe that scientists have found skeletons of a hobbit-like species of human that grew no larger than a three-year-old modern child? The tiny humans, who had skulls about the size of grapefruits, lived with pygmy elephants and Komodo dragons on a remote island in Indonesia 18,000 years ago.

Are there ancient references to a time when gods were masters of the earth, a pre-human period? Are there creation myths, similar to the Genesis story, about the origins of man in other antediluvian cultures?

J.R.R. Tolkien wrote in *The Silmarillion*, the legendary precursor to *The Lord of the Rings*, as to the genesis of Middle-earth, "There was Eru (God), the One, who in Arda is called Ilúvatar; and he made first the Ainur (Angels), the Holy Ones, that were the offspring of his thought, [5]and they were with him before aught else was made."[6]

Ilúvatar sounds very similar to the God of Genesis. He was the master of all and had legions of angels and it was he who created Elves and Man. But, Ilúvatar was a creation of Tolkien's imagination. Are there ancient records or texts that tell us about the beginning of our world? The Sumerians have left copper cylinder seals and transcripts that tell us a very interesting tale about a family of gods from Heaven. The Great Father of the Gods, the King of the Gods, was named AN or ANU. His realm was the expanse of the heavens, and his symbol was a star. In the Sumerian pictographic writing the sign of a star also stood for An, for "heaven," and for "divine being" or "God" (descended of An). The meaning of the symbol remained through the ages, as the script moved from the Sumerian pictographic to the cuneiform Akkadian, to the stylized Babylonian and Assyrian.

Anu's abode, and the seat of his Kingship, was in the heavens. That was where the other Gods of Heaven and Earth went when they needed individual advice or favor, or where they met in assembly to settle disputes among themselves or to reach major decisions.

The above passages are very similar to those found in the Bible and in creation myths from all over the world. The biggest difference may be that there is evidence to prove that this family of gods actually lived.

Could knowledge of our ancient heritage be communicated centuries, millennia later through simple folklore or oral tradition? Are we simply receptacles of genetic memory, vicariously reliving our forgotten history, through Tolkien's family of finely sculptured characters projected on the big screen or woven into the fabric of his stories.

It is my aim to search for evidence that supports the theory that there is more fact than fiction in *The Lord of the Rings*.

3

The Coming of Gods

In *The Lord of the Rings*, Tolkien weaves a story that on its surface is drastically different from the world we know. His Middle-earth contains, not only humans and animals but also, Elves, Dwarves, Orcs, Dragons and of course Hobbits. He has sorcerers, some of which are good and others that are evil. He even has an evil God, the Lord Sauron, who is immortal and has the ability to create Orcs and other creatures from the clay of the earth.

Many of us believe that our history began, just as the Bible states in the Book of Genesis with, "In the beginning God created the heavens and the earth. Now the earth was formless and empty, darkness was over the surface of the deep, and the Spirit of God was hovering over the waters." Most of us know the rest of the creation story through attending Sunday school classes or weekly church services. We know God created the Earth, including Man and rested on the seventh day.

J.R.R. Tolkien was an Oxford University professor of Anglo-Saxon and English language. He was also a devote Roman Catholic who believed in the one God of the Bible. Yet, when he imagined the setting and his cast of characters for his Middle-earth, he chose to write a story about one main God and a pantheon of minor gods.

Moviegoers and readers of *The Lord of the Rings* realize that Tolkien wrote more books than *The Lord of the Rings*. Most people also know that he wrote *The Hobbit*, the original tale of There and Back Again, that tells the story of how the hobbit Bilbo Baggins and his friend Gandalf the Gray, a wizard, left on an adventure with a company of dwarves to reclaim a valuable treasure guarded by the dragon Smaug. It was only Bilbo's friendship with Gandalf that convinced the hobbit to leave the Shire in the first place. It was on this adventure that Bilbo met Gollum in the dark under the mountains and found the "Ring of Power."

Middle-earth also has its creation story and Tolkien tells it complete in his precursor of *The Lord of the Rings*, *The Silmarillion*. This is the story of mankind rising up in rebellion against the gods.

In Tolkien's world of Middle-earth we find that the all-powerful One, who is called Ilúvatar, created the earth. Ilúvatar created the Ainur, the Holy Ones (angels), who were with him when there was nothing else. It was said that the Ainur were made of Ilúvatar's thought and he taught them music, and that this music was as a light that burned away the darkness that previously filled the void. Then Ilúvatar created the Secret Fire that burns still in the heart of the world.

Ilúvatar gave the Ainur a vision of the future, a vision of history yet to come. Many of them became bewitched by this glimpse and chose to enter the World and to labor hard to fulfill the dream that was promised by Ilúvatar.

As previously stated, Ilúvatar was the creator and like the One whom Christians call God was the maker of Heaven and Earth. From him all things proceed, and to him all things return. He is the beginning and the end, the Alpha and the Omega. He is the One who shapes all things.

The Elves knew of the Ainur and named the greatest of them Valar. They had the powers of the Arda (Earth) and men called them gods. They were similar to archangels and were treated with much adoration and reverence.

There were fourteen Valar, seven Lords and seven Queens. The Elves had special names for the Valar. The Lords were: Manwe, Ulmo, Aule, Orome, Mandos, Lorien and Tulkas; and the names of the Queens were: Varda, Yavanna, Nienna Este, Vaire, Vana and Nessa. Originally, there had been fifteen Valar, but because of Melkor's treachery his name is no longer spoken. Mankind also knew of the Valar and they gave them numerous names.

Tolkien used his religious upbringing to paint the origins of Middle-earth. The personification of Ilúvatar as the Lord God is almost identical to the Bible, especially in Genesis 1-5, "In the beginning God created the heavens and the earth. Now, the earth was formless and empty, darkness was over the surface of the deep and the Spirit of God was hovering over the waters. And God said, "Let there be light, "and there was light. God saw that the light was good, and he separated the light from the darkness. God called the light "day," and the darkness he called "night." And there was evening and there was morning—the first day."

It is my belief that Tolkien was inspired by the very earth histories and myths he taught. In Genesis 6:1-8, we read: "When men began to increase in number on the earth and daughters were born to them, the sons of God (angels) saw that the daughters of men were beautiful, and they married any of them they chose. Then the Lord said, "My Spirit will not contend with man forever for he is mortal, his days will be a hundred and twenty years."

The Nephilim (angels) were on the earth in those days—and also afterward—when the sons of God went to the daughters of men and had children by them. They were the heroes of old, men of renown. (Genesis 6:4)

In the Book of Enoch, we find the same story. For those unfamiliar with the Book of Enoch, here is a brief history. The book was originally part of the Bible until the fourth century. The Book existed centuries before the birth of Christ and yet is considered by many to be more Christian in its theology than Jewish. Many early Christians considered it scripture. The earliest literature of the so-called "Church Fathers" is filled with references to this mysterious book. The early second century "Epistle of Barnabus" makes much use of the Book of Enoch. Second and Third Century "Church Fathers" like Justin Martyr, Irenaeus, Origin and Clement of Alexandria all make use of the Book of Enoch. Tertullian (160-230 A.D.) even called the Book of Enoch "Holy Scripture." The Ethiopia Church added the Book of Enoch to its official canon. It was widely known and read the first three centuries after Christ. This and many other books became discredited after the Council of Laodicea. And being under ban of the authorities, afterwards it gradually passed out of circulation. The Council of Laodicea was held in 364 A.D.

The return of the long lost Book of Enoch to the modern western world is credited to the famous explorer James Bruce, who in 1773 returned from six years in Abyssinia with three Ethiopia copies of the lost book. In 1821 Richard Laurence published the first English translation. The famous R.H. Charles edition was published in 1912. In the following years several portions of the Greek text surfaced. Then with the discovery of cave 4 of the Dead Sea Scrolls, seven fragmentary copies of the Aramaic text were discovered. A group of angels that descended from heaven took human women as mates, "And all the others together with them took unto themselves wives, and each chose for himself one, and they began to go in unto them and to defile themselves with them, and they taught them charms and enchantments, and the cutting of roots, and made them acquainted with plants. And they became pregnant, and they bare great giants, whose height was three thousand ells: who consumed all the acquisitions of men. And when men could no longer sustain them, the giants turned against them and devoured mankind. And they began to sin against birds, and beasts, and reptiles, and fish, and to devour one another's flesh, and drink the blood. Then the earth laid accusation against the lawless ones."

Modern man has believed that civilization had its beginnings in ancient Rome or Greece; but Greek philosophers pointed to an earlier time and place as the origin of civilized man—Egypt. Napoleon's 1899 expedition to Egypt brought news of huge pyramids and ancient half buried temple-cities to the world. And the discovery of the Rosetta stone, written in Egyptian hieroglyphics as well as two known languages, seemed magically to pull the veil of ignorance from the eyes of scholars and suggested yet again to an even earlier civilization to be found in the Near East. The (Greek) Hellenic alphabet, which is the basis for both Latin and English languages, had its origin in the Near East. Even the Hebrew alphabet has the same number of letters and in the same order.

What all of this meant was that man could finally read and understand ancient texts dating back 4,000–5,000 BCE. With this knowledge, for the first time, Biblical stories could be collaborated using actual historical texts. Names and locations of ancient places could be found. Biblical Kings could be identified and their relationships with their gods and their peoples emphasized. (Note that Tolkien in *The Silmarillion* suggested that the timeline was approximately 6,000 years ago or 4,000 BCE.)

It is important to note that archaeologists began serious excavations of Sumer (Iraq) in the nineteenth century. They did this as a result of the discovery by scholars that Akkadian cuneiform script was syllabic—phonetic, but also made use of pictographs, not unlike hieroglyphs. What they had discovered was that Akkadian language was based on an entirely earlier language. Huge depositories of Akkadian texts were discovered in Nineveh. Indeed this ancient library contained 25,000 tablets.

> When in heights of heaven had not been named,
> And below, Earth had not been called;
> Nought, but primordial Apsu, their begetter,
> MUMMU and TIAMAT—she who bore them all,
> Their waters were mingled together.

This verse is the original pre-Genesis Creation myth: known to ancient Babylonians and Assyrians as the Enuma elish in accordance with the first words "When on high." It was first composed around 3,500 years ago, there do still exist versions from the first millennium BCE—the era from which the above extract is taken. The poet explains to us that in the beginning there was nothing but a watery dimension and that Apsu (male) was the 'sweet waters.' Mummu (male) was the 'veiling mist' and Tiamat (female) was the 'salt waters.' This is very similar to the Genesis story of the Bible, which tells us that God created dry land and that the earth was without form and void and darkness was upon the face of the deep.

Sir Austen Henry Layard was excavating the library of King Ashur-banipal at Nineveh when he discovered the first Enuma elish tablets. The excavations took place during the years 1848-76.

These tablets were translated and published by George Smith under the title *The Chaldean Account of Genesis.*

More examples of the Enuma elish have been discovered at Ashur, Kish and Uruk. It has also been ascertained that there is still earlier texts written in a more ancient language.

During the sixth century in Babylon it was normal for Nebuchadnezzar to have the Enuma elish recited during the New Year festivals as it had been for many centuries. At this time the Israelites were being held captive in Babylon and certainly witnessed if not participated in the eleven-day festival celebrating the creation of earth. There is little doubt that the Enuma elish influenced the creation myth of the Israelites, but there is still one major difference.

This poem informs us that the world was empty. There were no pastures or marshlands and the Gods had not yet been created. It states that because there were no beings on the earth no one had a name and therefore all destinies were open. And then suddenly, the gods arrived.[7]

According to Sumerian texts, the 'golden gods' were the gods of the epic tales and in the Sumerian belief; they had come down to Earth from Heaven. They were called the Anunnaki by some and also by the name Nephilim.

The head of the family of Gods of Heaven was AN (or Anu in the Babylonian/Assyrian texts). He was the Great Father of the Gods, the King of the Gods.

The second most powerful deity of the Sumerian pantheon was EN.LIL. His name meant "lord of the airspace", and he was the prototype and father of the later Storm Gods that were to head the pantheons of the ancient world.

Enlil (EN.LIL) was Anu's oldest son. He was born at his father's Heavenly Abode. He descended to Earth very early after the Anunnaki's arrival and was thus heralded as the principal God of Heaven and Earth. When the gods met in assembly at Anu's Heavenly Abode, Enlil presided over the meetings with his father and when the Gods met for assembly on Earth, they met at Enlil's court in the divine precinct of Nippur. Nippur was the city dedicated to Enlil and the site of his main temple, the K.KUR).[8]

Enlil also selected the kings who were to rule over Mankind, not as sovereigns but as servants of the God entrusted with the administration of divine laws of justice. Accordingly, Sumerian, Akkadian, and Babylonian kings opened their inscriptions of self-adoration by describing how Enlil had called them to Kingship. These 'calls' issued by Enlil on behalf of himself and his father Anu granted legitimacy to the ruler and outlined his functions. Even Hammurabi, who acknowledged a god named Marduk as the national God of Babylon, prefaced his code of laws by stating that "Anu and Enlil named me to promote the welfare of the people … to cause justice to prevail in the land."[9]

The third Great God of Sumer was another son of Anu; he bore two names, E.A. and EN.KI. Like his brother Enlil, he too, was a God of Heaven and Earth, a deity originally of the heavens, who had come down to earth.[10]

According to the Sumerian texts, including a truly amazing autobiography by Ea, he was born in the heavens and came down to Earth before there was any settlement or civilization upon the Earth. "When I approached the land, there was much flooding," he stated. He then proceeded to describe the series of actions taken by him to make the land habitable: he filled the Tigris River with fresh, "life-giving waters," he appointed a God to supervise the construction of canals, to make the Tigris and Euphrates navigable; and he unclogged the marshlands. He filled them up with fish and making them a haven for birds of all kinds, and causing to grow there (,) reeds that were a useful building material.[11]

Turning from the seas and rivers to the dry land, Ea claimed that it was he who "directed the plow and the yoke … opened the holy furrows … built the stalls … erected sheepfolds." Continuing, the self-adulatory text (named by scholars "Enki and the World Order") credited the god with bringing to Earth the arts of brick making, construction of dwellings and cities, metallurgy, and so on.[12] Not only the Sumerians but also the very Gods of Sumer considered Enlil supreme. They called him Ruler of All the Lands, and made it clear that "in Heaven—he is the Prince, On Earth—he is the Chief." His "word (command) high above made the Heavens tremble, down below made the Earth quake."

Enlil, according to Sumerian beliefs, arrived on Earth well before Earth became settled and civilized. A "Hymn to Enlil, the All-Beneficent" recounts the many aspects of society and civilization that would not have existed had it not been for Enlil's instructions to "execute his orders, far and wide."

One of the largest mysteries of ancient history is the origin of the Sumerians! Sir Leonard Woolley, one of the leading Sumerian archaeologists has been quoted as saying that they came, "whence we do not know."

Usually, the name of a people is associated with the name of the area or region where they live. But in this case the area was called Sumer because the Sumerians settled there. To be more precise, the word Sumer comes from and is unique to the Sumerian language, so it is more accurate to say that the people are Sumerian speaking.

The original question still begs an answer. The Sumerians seem to have just appeared on the scene, as if they had just arrived ... and they were much more advanced technologically and academically than their neighbors. In fact, their equal could not be found on earth 6000 years ago.

When tablets were first discovered in the 19th century written in the Sumerian language scholars were puzzled because the writings did not resemble Semitic or Indo-European. It bore no relation to Arabic, Jewish, Canaanite, Phoenician, Syrian, Assyrian, Persian, Indian, Egyptian, nor to any language from the European, African or Asian continents. To quote Professor Kramer, the Sumerian language "stands alone and unrelated to any known language living or dead."[13]

A clay tablet has been unearthed, written by King Ashur-banipal of Assyria, in 700 BCE that stated: "The God of the scribes has bestowed upon me the gift of the knowledge of his art. I have been initiated into the secrets of writing. I can even read the intricate tablets in Sumerian. I understand the enigmatic words in the stone carvings from the days before the Flood."[14]

Another example of Gods coming to Earth can be found in the Dogon mythology. The Dogon who claim to be originally from Egypt now live in an isolated mountainous region of Bandiagara, south of the Sahara Desert in Mali, West Africa. They were one of the last people to lose their independence and come under French rule. The Dogon were perceived as being the best example of "primitive savagery" known to the world at that time.

The Dogon claim that their Gods, the Nummo, arrived from the sky in a vessel that landed with great noise and wind. After landing, in a vessel with four legs, they dragged it into a hollow, which they filled with water until the vessel floated. The Nummo are described as being very different physically from humans. Ogotemmeli, who was the oral historian of the Dogon tribe, said that the Nummo's physical characteristics reminded him of a fish or a snake. Yet, he believed that they were far superior in intelligence to humans. According to oral tradition the Nummo change the Earth animals, who are "naked and speechless," by combining their DNA with that of the animals. The lack of intelligence on the Earth is identified as "disorder" that the Nummo want to end. By combining their DNA with the Earth animals they bring order to the universe.[15]

As we have seen, the creation story featured of the Bible may have been inspired by a multitude of interventions of gods. It is through this maze of fact and faith that Man's earliest history is derived.

Tolkien speaks of his God in relationship to his writings, "We have come from God and inevitably the myths woven by us, though they contain error, will also reflect a splintered fragment of the true light, the eternal truth that is with

God. Indeed, only by myth-making, only by becoming a "sub-creator" and inventing stories, can Man ascribe to the state of perfection that he knew before the fall." [16]

We are just at the beginning stages of understanding that there is far more to our history than we have been told. Tolkien's tapestries of tales seem to have been woven of alternating threads from his religious and historical perspectives.

4

The Coming of Elves

The Lord of the Rings demonstrates how important the Elves were in the hierarchy of Middle-earth because it was they that received the first three rings of power.

It is not mere coincidence that the first three rings were given to the Elven-kings. They were the favorites and the first race created by the gods and when they looked skyward the dark canopy of the heavens was studded with stars.

They lived for a long time under the stars exploring their homeland and beyond and began naming things they saw. They called themselves the Quendi. When they were created the elves were much stronger and greater than they came to be, but they also became fairer. Indeed, "for though the beauty of Quendi in the days of their youth was beyond all other beauty that Ilúvatar has caused to be, it has not perished, but lives in the West, and sorrow and wisdom have enriched it."

Tolkien writes that the Elves remain until the end of time and do not die until the world dies. Their strength will not diminish and they can only be killed in battle. They will live for 10,000 centuries and then they will be called to the halls of Mandos in Valinor. It also states that the Elves shall join Men in the Second Music of Ainur. This is similar to the second coming of Christ as it relates to the aftermath—the final judgment after the one thousand years of peace.

It is told that the Valar, who had for so long had waited, finally found the original Children of Ilúvatar, almost by chance. Orome of the Valar (Gods' helpers), after the Quendi had been found was said to he filled with wonder. Now, Orome loved the Quendi, and named them in their own tongue Eldar, 'the people of the stars.'

Elrond was the Lord of Rivendell and mighty among both Elves and Men. He was ageless, neither young nor old. It was said he could remember things long past, both happy and sad. He had dark hair but it gave way to a circle of silver. His gray eyes were clear and it was said they sparkled like stars. On one hand he looked mature and seasoned, perhaps a little too seasoned, but on the other he reminded you of a battle-hardened warrior full of zest for life and war. Elrond was truly an august king.

Can we find proof of elves or elf-lords in our ancient past?

Yes, we find the origins of the Elves, also called the 'Shining Ones', dating back some 5000 years to ancient Mesopotamia (Iraq). Christian and Barbara Joy O'Brien have conducted some of the best modern research into the etymological roots of the long distant BCE years. They spent many years, as exploration geologists in Iran, where they were involved in the discovery of the Tchoga Zambil ziggurat. This Tower to the Sky was the pride of the ancient city of Dur Untash and its king Untash-gal (Untash the Great) in the land of the Elamites.

Artist's illustration of a typical Ziggurat.

Since 1970 the O'Brien's have concentrated their research into the many enigmas of prehistory, and have written some excellent books. In their book Genius of the Few, they explain that the ancient word El which was identified as meaning a God or lofty-one (as in El Elyon and El Shaddai) actually meant "Shining" in old Mesopotamian Sumer. Just to see how widespread the use of the translated name Elf truly was all we have to do is look at its various roots in these areas: Ellyl in Wales, Aillil in Ireland, Aelf in Saxony and Elf in England. The plural of El was Elohim. This word was used in old biblical texts to denote the gods. Ironically, this plurality was overlooked and mistranslated to add weight to the Judaeo-Christian claims of the 'One God.' Even more interesting is the fact that in Gaelic Cornwall, South West England, the word el means literally in Anglo-Saxon engel and the old French word angele in English becomes 'angel'.

Archaeological science has broadened its base to cover many new and exciting disciplines including the spread of agriculture, pastoralism—social and economic system based on the raising and herding of livestock, genetics and language, which take us to Southern Lebanon before 8,000 BCE. Here, we discover our ancestors and can see their agrarian efforts flourish transforming our planet into a horn of plenty.

It was only during the reign of Queen Victoria that archaeological evidence came to light, by the discovery of thousands of clay tablets inscribed with 'cuneiform' text (wedge shaped lines) recovered, of a cultured and ordered Sumerian civilization, which was in full flower more than 2000 years before the old testament Bible stories were compiled between 850 BCE and 550 BCE.

The Shining Ones of the Elohim (as indicated in Sumerian writings from as far back as the 3rd millennium BCE) were identified with the skies or with a high place described as An and often translated to mean Heaven (or the heavens). In this context, the great gods and overlords of ancient Sumer were called the Anunnaki (Anun-na-ki meaning: 'Heaven came to earth'). For this reason, it was traditionally referred to as the Elven Bloodline or the dynasty of the Shining Ones.

It is becoming ever clearer that the Anunnaki were not confined to the Mesopotamian region; neither did they make their only appearance in the Sumerian culture, as we shall discover.

The Anunnaki seem to have arrived upon history sometime prior to the Sumerian era, approximately 5500 BCE. …

The importance of the Elf-Queens of the matrilineal royal bloodline dates back thousands of years to the time of the great Anunnaki Lord of the Sky, Anu. His life is documented on clay tablets and cylinder seals from the 3rd millennium BCE. The clay tablets and cylinder seals were discovered in the Sumerian delta eden of the Persian Gulf. Anu's queenly consorts were his sisters: Antu, Lady of the Sky, and Ki, the Earth Mother. Anu had two sons: Enlil (whose mother was Ki), and Enki (whose mother was Antu). Enki had two wives, one of whom was his half-sister Nin-khursag, the Lady of Life. By the same token, Enlil similarly had two wives, including Ninkhursag who was, therefore, consort to each of her brothers. This heavenly family descended from the great Mother Goddess Tiamat and is described in the Enuma Elish as "She who bore them all."

On October 30, 2000, Iraqi archaeologists reported uncovering an ancient Sumerian 'city of graves'. The archaeologists are striving to bring to light what they describe as Mesopotamia's largest "city of graves," where Sumerians buried their dead almost 5,000 years ago. The size of the cemetery is monumental and scientists say much more work needs to be done to determine what role it played in ancient times.

"We have never excavated anything like it before. It is unprecedented," says Fadhil Abdulwahid, a Baghdad University archaeologist. The burial site is in a remote and desolate area, and was overrun with scorpions. The locals named the area Umm al-Ajarib or "Mother of Scorpions." It was hoped that the majority of the graves would be left undisturbed, but this did not prevent grave robbers from carrying away gold ornaments, cylinder seals made of precious stones and statuettes. Traditionally ancient Iraqis buried their dead with their valued possessions.

Shells, bowls, beads, earthenware and statues dot small lanes in the cemetery, situated 400 km south of Baghdad. "It is the largest graveyard of Sumer. Nowhere in ancient Iraq have we come across so many graves," Chief archaeologist Donny Youkhanna said.

Ancient Iraqis were buried in coffins of brick laid in bitumen as mortar. These graves were regularly arranged, like today's modern cemeteries. Funerary rituals were very important to Iraqis. They believed that if the dead were not buried properly that their souls would return and haunt living relatives.

Believe it or not, after a Sumerian king conquered a city, the first thing he would do was open the graves. This was done to release the souls, so that they would chase away any enemy soldiers not killed in the battle for the city. …

Elf Lords and Elf Queens played a major role during the middle ages. In fact, one of the most famous families of the time was the Plantagenets. They were patrons of Geoffrey Chaucer, the father of English poetry. During the early part of the period, the architectural style of the Normans gave way to the Gothic, in which style Salisbury Cathedral was built. Westminster Abbey was rebuilt and the majority of English cathedrals remodeled. The Plantagenets were a junior branch of the House of Anjou, whose senior branch was the House of Vere. Indeed in 1861, the noted royal historian Baron Thomas Babington Macaulay described the Veres as "the longest and most illustrious line of nobles that England has ever seen. Their ancestry was jointly Pictish and Merovingian, descending from the ancient Grail House of Scythia. Here was a true kingly line of the Elven Race, and it was for this reason the Oberon (a variant of Aubrey/ Abrey, the historical Elf King) became Shakespeare's King of the Fairies."

The Lord Chancellor of England in the 16th century was Edward de Vere. He had followed in the footsteps of his ancestors and continued the family line of Lord Chancellors, which had begun with Aubrey, the 12th century Prince of Anjou, and Guisnes, whose titular name, Albe-Righ, meant Elf King.

Elizabeth I sat on the English throne when Edward de Vere was the Lord Chancellor of England. She was known as the Tudor Queen. Of all the monarchs who sat upon the English throne, she was by far the most in step with the ancient cultures and the wood lore. Before she was formally crowned, she was known as the Faerie Queene and was recognized by the people as the Queen of the Green-wood. The Elven Race of the Albigens performed this ancient ritual of the Shin-ing Ones, also. The ceremony was conducted in the mist of early dawn in the depths of Windsor Forest and to facilitate the installation, the customary Robin Hood legacy of the House of Vere was brought into play. At that time, the Queen's Lord Chamberlain was Edward de Vere of Loxley, 17th Earl of Oxford, and it was his office to invest Elizabeth by first deposing the Caille Daouine. This was the traditional King of the Forest (whose name had given rise to Scotland's Pictish realm of Caledonia)—the mighty Stag of the Seven Tines, upon whose back Lord Vere rode into the ceremonial clearing.

Fountains, springs, and water have always been associated with the female line of the Ring Lords. In ancient Mesopotamia writings tell of the founding mother of the Anunnaki, Tiamat, who was known as the Sea-Dragon. Since that time, these queens have been represented as mermaids or as ladies of the lake. Mary Magdalene, as one of the females of the Ring Lords, when she arrived in Provence in 44 A.D., was accorded this right.

You probably don't believe you have seen or heard of Elf-queens prior to *The Lord of the Rings*. If this were your belief then you would be wrong. Have you read or watched the stories about Cinderella, Robin Hood, Sleeping Beauty, or Rapunzel? All of these stories have one common theme, which is to save the "damsel in distress", or Elf-Queen. The Grail Kings could not continue their bloodline without the Grail Queen. If the "knight in shining armor" was unsuc-cessful in saving the damsel than their royal seed could not be passed on to the next generation. The majority of these tales are thousands of years old and were written by unknown authors. The Catholic Church with the fabrication of the Donation of Constantine tried to eliminate or twist the original tales so as to minimize the role of the Grail Kings or the Grail Bloodline. We will explore the Donation of Constantine later in this book, but its purpose was to de-legitimize the "Divine Right of Kings" and to give legitimacy to the Church's claim of being the only earthly power able to bestow kingship. The Church would now create kings and queens based entirely on its political agenda, as easily as it ordained priests, ignoring established rights of succession through royal blood.

What did these Elf Kings and Queens look like? Various sites around the world have been excavated and based on their preserved remains and personal artifacts we now know that the men were at least six foot six inches, and the woman were over six feet tall. They had light brown to red hair, pale eyes, were leather clad and lived in a vast world that stretched from Transylvania to Tibet! History now teaches us that these forebears of the Gaelic and Celtic High Kings were among the most awesome warriors of all history … The Elves or Elf-Lords may very well be the result of a failed DNA experiment.

Amphibious aliens came to earth with "great noise and wind", according to Ogotemmeli, a member of the Dogon tribe. Like his father before him, he was responsible for remembering and reciting the oral history of his tribe. He must pass this knowledge on to his heir to ensure that thousands of years of history are not forgotten on the winds of time. These amphibious aliens were the Nummo and were often compared to "serpents, lizards, chameleons and occasionally sloths, because they were slow moving and having a shapeless neck. They were also identified as being fish capable of walking on land. While they were on land, the Nummo stood upright on their tails. Most descriptions indicate the Nummo's skin was primarily green but that is sometimes changed similar to that of a chameleon and was described at times as having all the colors of the rainbow."

They discovered that the Earth animals were "naked and speechless", that is they had not evolved to the point where they could reason and speak! This perceived lack of intelligence was identified as "disorder", and the Nummo planned to change that. By combining their DNA with the Earth animals they brought order to the universe. The animals referred to are Men. As a result of this new-order Man learns to speak and becomes clothed.

Good plan but bad execution. The first experiments failed. These aliens didn't take into consideration the problems of combining their androgynous (both male and female) DNA with the DNA of single sexed animals (humans).

According to Ogotemmeli the first biological experiment, which involved a union between Nummo and Mother Earth, resulted in two types of human/ Nummo hybrids being born. One type of offspring was born normal like the Nummo, meaning that this being was an androgynous or a "twin" Nummo. The other offspring was born defective and was a single-sexed male known as "the jackal." Throughout the mythology references to twins are in fact references to self-fertilizing androgyny. Even though the "twin" Nummo are identified as being self-fertilizing androgynous beings, there are references to the fact that the Dogon people perceived them as being feminine.

Intelligence in any creature is determined by its ability to communicate. According to Lilly, "ape's brains are limited in size, three hundred to four hundred fifty grams. When humans are born and become adults with brains restricted to these sizes they are unable to use spoken language adequately to function in our society. To master speech as we know it, humans apparently require a brain size of at least seven hundred to eight hundred grams." This could be why in Dogon mythology the key figures in the mythology is the "seventh" ancestor who becomes "the Master of Speech". The reference to the number seven may be symbolic of the seventh ancestor having a brain size of 700 grams.

In this first attempt at biological engineering, the androgynous aspects of the Nummo did not carry through to both of the offspring. Ogotemmeli explained how "the original incident was destined to affect the course of things forever; from this defective union there was born, instead of the intended twins, a single being, the Thos aureus or jackals symbol of the difficulties of God. With the first offspring, the Dogon perceive the androgynous human/Nummo hybrid as being feminine and good, while the brother of this being the jackal, who is a single-sexed male, is perceived as being soulless.

The mythology indicates that the reason the experiment failed was because the Nummo neglected to take into account the problems of combining their androgynous DNA with the DNA of single sexed animals. They were also unaware that their spiritual essence was connected with their biological essence and by tampering with one it affected the other.

The jackal is a symbol of the failed biological experiment. As a result of his birth, the Nummo have to recreate the DNA to try to correct the mistake. In the end, most of the Nummo DNA is removed from humans and humans eventually lose their immortality and consequently their understanding of truth and immortality. Because of this, the jackal becomes symbolic of death in humanity.

The androgynous human/Nummo hybrid of the first experiment is feminine and good. According to the mythology, the Nummo were perceived as being immortal, meaning that when they died and were reborn they were able to remember their previous existence. Immortality in this sense is what we know of as reincarnation. They were also able to connect with each other and other animals and plants on a level that is unknown to humans. The jackal, as a result of not being immortal, was cursed with always being alone.

The Nummo were said to resemble amphibians, reptiles, or serpents. It may not be a coincidence that the Bible describes Satan as being a serpent, when he encouraged Adam and Eve to partake of the fruit from the tree of knowledge of good and evil. It was only after eating the fruit that they realized that they were naked and covered themselves. Could these covers also relate in some way to the fibrous skirt in the Dogon mythology? They were also told that if they ate the fruit they would die. Is this when Man lost his immortality and was cursed to die?

The Nummo, although androgynous, procreate by having intercourse just like the gendered humans and the human/Nummo hybrids. The Dogon people saw the Nummo as a race of gods and the Nummo like the God of the Bible wanted Man to use sex as a means of procreation in order to provide diversity to the gene pool.

It seems the gods did not want Man to have knowledge or enjoyment of sex. It has been this "sin" of the wise that has corrupted Man since time began. It is also responsible, at least in part, for all the stories of lost and forbidden love.

5

The Coming of Dwarves

When Frodo and Sam were in Rivendell they found themselves seated around Elrond's table where important people and members of the Fellowship of the Ring were gathered. Next to Frodo on his right sat an important looking dwarf who was richly dressed. He had a very long and forked beard. It was white, nearly as white as the snow-white cloth of his garments. He also wore a silver belt, and around his neck hung a chain of silver and diamonds. Frodo was so taken with the dwarf that he stopped eating to look at him. Welcome and well met," said the dwarf, turning towards him. He raised himself from the table and bowed, adding "Gloin at your service."

This was Frodo's first experience with Dwarves and he was most amazed to be meeting Gloin, one of the twelve companions of the great Thorin Oakenshield.

Tolkien informs us that dwarves weren't created as much as forged in the fires of the mountains. They were natural deep-delving miners, masons, metalworkers and the most artistic stone-carvers. They grew long beards and stood four to five feet in height, but they lived a long life averaging 250 years.

Aule, of the Valar, created the dwarves. He was a God, an angel, and he loved all things. He did not tell Ilúvatar of his creations and hid their location. Ilúvatar knew about the dwarves and asked Aule, "Why hast thou done this?" So Aule answered, "I desired things other than I am, to love and to teach them, so they too might perceive the beauty of Ea, which thou has caused to be."

The origin of Dwarves is typically traced to the legends of ancient mythology. Gaelic and Norman peoples carried their traditions to the British Isles.

They are short, usually bearded and appear to be very old. Their aged appearance seems to be caused by the fact that they reach maturity at age three.

Dwarves lived mainly in the mountains of Scandinavia and worked in mines in Germany. They prefer residing in communities rather than to live solitary lives. Mountain dwarves have established elaborate organization to order their lives. They have unique kingdoms and an orderly bloodline of royal kings. They are famous for their weaponry and the fierceness of their armies. The Elves call them the Sidhe or Shee (Gaelic for "people of the hills"). One of their favorite indulgences in life is drinking, both mead and beer, of which they were master brewers.

Dwarves have been confused with Goblins and Gnomes for years. If you remember the Goblins were evil in *The Hobbit* and in *The Lord of the Rings*. So for your information Goblins are a very different, more grotesque variety of gnomes. They are known to be playful, but at other times they are evil, and their tricks could seriously harm people. A goblin smile is said to curdle the blood and a goblin's laugh can sour the milk. It is even said that goblins cause fruit to fall from trees. They pester humans by hiding small objects, tipping over pails of milk and changing or hiding signposts.

Goblins originated in France and spread rapidly all over Europe. They have no homes and usually live in mossy clefts in rocks and roots of ancient trees, although they never stay very long in the same place. The name 'hobgoblin' is thought to be an abbreviation of 'Robin Goblin', the name Druids gave to the first goblins when they entered Britain.

It seems that we all have been genetically altered, regardless if we believe the creation myths of the Bible, of the Anunnaki, the Nummo or of Tolkien himself. Over the last six thousand years many races have intermarried into other races. Therefore it should not be too incredible to believe that a tall dwarf man could have married a short human woman or vise versa.

Artist's impression of genetic mix of fish and a lion.

All dwarves could have carried the gene responsible for creating dwarfism, where it was perfectly normal. Through intermarriage, it could be concluded that this gene was passed into and made part of the human DNA and as a result occasionally dwarves were born due to this inheritance of the gene.

Today dwarves are born into the families of normal height parents. The only apparent reason for this is a faulty gene. There are more than 200 recognized conditions which cause dwarfism. Most of them are genetic and can result from either a spontaneous genetic change (mutation) or by inheriting the gene from one or both parents.

Both spontaneous genetic change and inherited genes can cause two average-size parents to have a child of shorter stature. The most common form of dwarfism in children is called achondroplasia: 85% are born to average-size parents. Dwarfism plays no favorites and occurs in all ethnic groups.

Spontaneous genetic change of a single normal gene in a chromosome passed to the child by the parent can cause this condition. Scientists are aware of several causes of genetic mutation e.g. radioactivity, chemicals and viruses. If the parent's DNA carries the dwarfism gene, the offspring will undoubtedly inherit the condition.

Spontaneous mutation can occur in any pregnancy and is the more frequent cause of a child with dwarfism being born to average-size parents.

If both parents carry a recessive gene that produces dwarfism, and they both pass that gene to their child, the child would be of short stature. This means they possess the gene that causes the condition but do not actually have the condition themselves.

Dwarves seem to be very similar in appearance if not in manner to Hobbits. The next chapter delves into the origins and history of the Hobbits and will inform you about a recent Hobbit discovery.

6

The Coming of Hobbits

Hobbits have been discovered by scientists, and by their very discovery indicate that Man did exist with other humanlike species. Scientists have determined that this species, named Homo floresiensis, is completely new to science. Dig workers dubbed the tiny human as the "hobbit," after the tiny creatures from *The Lord of the Rings* books.

"The hobbit was nobody's fool," Roberts said. "They survived alongside us [Homo Sapiens] for at least 30,000 years, and were not known for being very amiable eco-companions. And the hobbits were managing some extraordinary things-manufacturing sophisticated stone tools, hunting pygmy elephants, and crossing at least two water barriers to reach Flores from mainland Asia-with a brain only one-third the size of ours."

J.R.R. Tolkien's Hobbits may have evolved from the species reported above. How do they relate to the hobbits we know and love?

Hobbits were an unobtrusive but very ancient people. They were more numerous formerly than they are today for they love peace and quiet and well tilled earth: a well-ordered and well-farmed countryside was their favorite haunt. They do not and did not understand or like machines more complicated than a forge-bellows, a water mill, or a handloom, though they were skillful with tools. Even in ancient days they were, as a rule, shy of the 'Big Folk', as they called us. Even now they try to avoid and dismay us and are becoming hard to find.

We find this description of hobbits: hobbits really are little people, smaller even than of Dwarves, with average heights of between two and three feet tall. They were taller in the olden days growing as much as four feet in height. There is one report that Bandobras Took, son of Isengrim the Second was actually four foot five and rode horses.

We also read that hobbits originally lived in holes in the ground, but this was years ago. Today, only the very rich or the very poor actually live in holes in the ground. The rich have spacious homes built into the sides of hills with tunnels leading to decorate and comfortable rooms. Their homes are well lit by large windows and each has a large round door for an entrance with a single doorknob positioned exactly in its center. The poor live in little more than dirt burrows scratched out of the ground, lucky to even have one window.

Most Hobbits live in farmhouses and even have barns. The land surrounding the Shire was mostly flat and not suitable for many hillside homes. So the people of the Shire lived like most people of the era in normal homes built above the ground. Although, with the passing of the Third Age of Middle-earth long past, the shape of all lands has been changed by time and war. But the lands of the Hobbits are probably where they always were—Northwest of the Old World, east of the Sea.

Tolkien wrote that the hobbits originated in the Valley of Anduin, between Mirkwood and the Misty Mountains. According to *The Lord of the Rings*, the hobbits have lost their genealogical details, and therefore did not know how they are related to humankind. By the end of the Third Age there were three types of Hobbits, all with different temperaments. The Harfoots were by far the largest clan and were Frodo's people. The Stoors lived near water and enjoyed boats and swimming. The Fallohides were a smaller later clan, and like Bilbo had an adventurous streak.

According to The Concise Oxford Dictionary of Current English: "hobbit n. one of an imaginary race of half-sized persons in stories by Tolkien; hence ~RY (5) n. [invented by J.R.R. Tolkien, Engl. writer d. 1973, and said by him to mean 'hole-builder']".

A search of early English sources for the word 'hobbit' has turned up the possible root word. The word is hob, which means 'sprite' or 'little man', as in hob-goblin. Another root maybe the Old English words hol byldan, which means 'to build a hole'. It's easy to see how this phrase could have evolved over millennia to the noun 'hobbit'. The modern Dictionary has reverted to the more strictly accurate "hole-builder."

When you Google the phrase 'origin hobbit' you are bombarded with over 100,000 results. By clicking on some of links near the top you will eventually be lead to the following. "The only source known today that makes reference to hobbits in any sort of historical context is the Denham Tracts by Michael Aislabie Denham. This is a long list of sprites and bogies, based on an older list, the Discovery of Witchcraft, dated 1584. Denham copied this list, and added a great number of names to it, including 'boggleboes', 'freiths', 'wirrikows', and 'hobbits'. While many feel there is good reason to suspect that Denham invented the word himself, others feel it's more likely that the word was highly obscure at the time, and became virtually non-existent due to lack of use. Some believe this may have been the "fairy tale" that the Habit had referred to in the 1938 letter."

Claims that 'Little People' have existed in northern Europe have been prevalent throughout history. They have countless names for their wee folk including: brownies, pixies, fays, leprechauns, gnomes and troglodytes. Some people believe that these beings are far more than just myth or folklore. There are those that think the 'Little People' interact with regular folk and sometimes help determine the outcome of certain events.

Take, for example, the Isle of Man in the middle of the Irish Sea: an island with a severe fairy infestation. In the southern parts of the island is the 'Fairy Bridge', a bridge that no man would cross without greeting the Little People that live there. To most, of course, this is just superstition, but there are those who believe that they share their island with all manner of fairy creatures. Among these is a being known as a phynnodderee who are shy of humans, friendly and happy-go-lucky, hairy-legged, fond of wine and beer and given to farm-work. Sound familiar?

7

The Coming of Man

In 1953, the husband and wife team of Ralph and Rose Solecki while searching for evidence of early man discovered a cave in Kurdistan, Iraq that contained nine ancient skeletons, four of which had been crushed by a rock fall. The cave situated at an altitude of 745 meters was named Shanidar by the archaeologists. Shanidar Cave is just one of many caves that honeycomb the Zagros Mountains. (According to the Bible, once Man was banished from the Garden of Eden he settled in the east, in the Zagros Mountains, bordering on the Mesopotamia plain.)

Today, Kurdish tribesmen use the caves for shelter and protection, against weather and war. (The discoveries found in the Shanidar Cave formed the basis for the popular novel by Jean Auel entitled *The Clan of the Cave Bear*. The novel was also made into a movie in 1986, starring Darryl Hannah as a young Cro-Magnon woman raised by Neanderthals.)

On a cold, winter night, 44,000 years ago, a family sought shelter in the Shanidar Cave. Sometime during the night the cave suffered a rock-fall crushing the entire family. Seven of these, including a baby, appeared to belong to a single family who had huddled together from the cold of winter. When the cave was discovered their team of archaeologists cleared away layer after layer of debris and what they uncovered was the time-line of man in this geographic area dating from as early as 10,000 years ago back to 100,000 years ago.

What this history showed was shocking. Man's culture had not shown a natural progression, as one would have expected using the Darwinian model of evolution, but over the 90,000-year period, Man's culture had actually regressed. According to their findings, from about 27,000 years BCE to about 11,000 years BCE man's culture had regressed and its population had dropped to a point near extinction.

Then suddenly everything changed. About 11,000 years ago "modern man" reappeared and culturally was more advanced than ever.

What could have happened during this time period that could explain such an amazing transformation? According to the archaeological record, man's population was dwindling and his technology had all but disappeared. One of the causes cited for this decline was the arrival of the last ice age, which started about 70,000 years ago and ended about 10,000 years ago. Prior to this re-emergence, man survived by hunting animals and eating fruit and vegetables where they grew, either from trees or fields.

Somehow, man seemed to gain knowledge. When Adam and Eve were expelled from the Garden of Eden, Adam had to toil hard to grow his food. "By the sweat of thy brow shalt thou eat bread", the Lord said to Adam. Years later, the Bible informs us that, "Abel was a keeper of herds and Cain was a tiller of the soil". Man had thus learned to shepherd herds and to grow a variety of crops including millet, rye, spelt, edible cereals, flax and a variety of fruit-bearing shrubs and trees. All of this knowledge came out of the Near East. Did the Bible start as stated above only 10,000 years ago? Did God or the Tree of Knowledge teach man how to survive?

Or was there another intervention?

Two skulls were discovered in an abandoned mine near a small rural village 100 miles southwest of Chihuahua, Mexico. A teenage Mexican girl found the skulls, sixty to seventy years ago, who was on a quest of discovery of exploring local caves and mines. At the back of one of the mine tunnels she found a complete human skeleton, which was lying on top of and not buried in the soil. Next to the body, an apparently misshapen skeletal hand was protruding out of the dirt. The hand was clasping one of the arms of the adult skeleton. The girl began to dig and soon was witness to the bones of what appeared to be a deformed child.

She decided to collect only the skulls and kept them for the remainder of her life. Eventually the skulls became the property of an American gentleman who passed them on to another couple. They decided to have the skulls examined and this is where the amazing part of the story begins.

They contacted Lloyd Pye who is now the caretaker of the skulls. He has named the child's skull the StarChild. Lloyd is a former intelligence officer in U.S. Military Intelligence and has been investigating the skull since 1998. He is also a pioneer in the field of discovering the truth of Man's development on this planet. He believes that evolution cannot explain how Homo sapiens suddenly evolved and became intelligent beings when they supposed ancestors were still living in trees.

One of the first things Pye did was to determine the age of the skulls. Scientists dated the skulls at 900 years old. The adult skull was that of a female and DNA testing proved it was not related to the infant. What really set them apart was the shape of their skulls. Although the skulls were approximately the same size they exhibited a huge difference in brain capacity. The child's brain cavity was much larger than that of its adult companion. The volume in a normal human skull is 1400 cubic centimeters but the StarChild's volume was 1600 cc! Scientists projected that if the child had lived to become an adult its brain capacity would have grown to 1800 cc or more.

Next, he had laboratories try to determine the genetic makeup of the child. They successfully found the mother's or matrilineal DNA but could not determine the father's. The markers for the father's DNA were eroded, so claim the technicians. Interestingly, the markers they looked for and the only markers the testing equipment was able to determine would have been human DNA. So we are left with the question: was there really no male DNA present or was there no human DNA present. This problem is being addressed and science is looking for methods to discover other types of humanoid DNA.

Pye believes that the cone shaped skulls discovered in Central and South America may also have enlarged brain capacity which may prove that the StarChild was not a freak of nature but one of many genetically altered humans.

Charles Darwin claimed that Mankind was related to the great apes. Today, this means we are distantly related to the orangutan, gorilla, and chimpanzee. All of these apes have 24 pairs of chromosomes. That is the female has 24 pairs of chromosomes in her egg and the male has 24 pairs of chromosomes in his sperm.

Lloyd Pye's research claims that humans have only 23 pairs of chromosomes and he states that this is truly remarkable because we once had 24 pairs of chromosomes just like the great apes. His research has discovered that our second and third chromosomes have been fused together and that this fusing could only be accomplished in a laboratory by manipulating the egg. No disease or natural genetic condition has ever caused a species to alter its chromosomal structure.

One possible explanation for this amazing fact is that a species with only 23 pairs of chromosomes wanted to procreate with another species with 24 pairs of chromosomes. The only way they could accomplish this was to fuse two chromosomes together. If they had simply removed one chromosome they would have changed the entire creature, but by fusing the chromosomes together they kept the creature intact and did not loose any of its genetic information.

I found an interesting website with a section entitled "Ask A Scientist", located at http://www.newton.dep.anl.gov/askasci/gen01/gen01739.htm. This particular section is dedicated to providing answers to questions that are not easily found on the Internet! It also should be mentioned that this is intended for K-12 teachers and students!

One student asked why apes and man haven't propagated. Why, if both apes and man descended from the same ancestor were there no offspring of a mating pair?

The expert replying to the student was Scott J. Badham and his answer supports the examples given but explains the number of genes were as a result of mutations not manipulations. He explains, "For instance, humans and chimpanzees have about 98.5% of our DNA in common. But humans have 46 chromosomes and chimps have 48. If you take the chromosomes of a chimp and those of a human and pair them up together, i.e. their number 1 by our number 1, and so on, it appears that somewhere chimp chromosome #2 split into 2 giving them an extra pair. If you pair our number 2 and the two halves of whichever one of theirs that split (I'm sorry I can't remember which ones!) the pattern of bands on both match up almost perfectly. (There are actually some other mutations that have also happened in this pair). The fact that humans have 46 and chimps have 48 makes it so our species cannot mate together anymore. Most species have different chromosome numbers and even if they are the same the genes that are on each chromosome might be different. Sometimes related organisms that are different species can reproduce together but their offspring can't mate, i.e. they are sterile. A good example of this is the offspring of the donkey and the horse, which is called a mule. One has 62 chromosomes and one has 64. This gives the mule 63, an uneven number. Dogs and wolves can have offspring that are fertile and for this reason some scientists argue that they really shouldn't be classified as separate species, but we may be witnessing a speciation event in progress. Another reason organisms speculate is due to geographic isolation. Once organisms can't get to each other to mate, over time they get different mutations in their DNA and adapt differently to their environments. If enough time passes and enough mutation has happened in theory they may not be able to mate again."

There is a history of genetic manipulation on this planet and remarkably the manipulators wrote down how they did it. It is included in their creation stories and begins with the third great God of Sumer Ea, who was born in the heavens and came down to Earth. According to Ea, there weren't any settlements or signs of civilization on Earth. "When I approached the land, there was much flooding," he stated. Ea then realized that he had to make the land habitable, so he filled Tigris River with fresh, life-giving waters and had canals constructed. The

Tigris and Euphrates rivers were made navigable, fish were introduced to the waters and reeds were planted that were useful as building material.

Turning from the seas and rivers to the dry land, Ea claimed that it was he who "directed the plow and the yoke ... opened the holy furrow ... built the stalls ... erected sheepfolds." He also takes credit for bringing to Earth the arts of brick making, construction of dwellings and cities, metallurgy, and so on.

8

The Coming of Kings

The Steward of Gondor was charged with the protection and guardianship of Minas Tirith and the City of Gondor. Basically, he was a glorified property manager waiting for the return of the rightful king.

The eldest of the woman who worked in the House of the Healing said, "The hands of the king are the hands of a healer. And so the rightful king could ever be known."

The Divine Right of Kings was much more than a chapter in a high school history book. It did not mean, as is often implied, that the King or Queen ruled because they were stronger, richer and smarter than their subjects. In fact, it had nothing to do with ruling over anyone or anything. True Kingship was and is in the blood. To be precise this royal bloodline can only be found in mitochondria DNA and is carried by the females. Ascension to a throne is therefore by inheritance only.

The Grail Kings of the Sumerians, the Pharaohs of Egypt, the Davidic Kings of Judah, the Dragon Kings of Scythia and the Fisher Kings of Gaul were all Kings that had given kingship to serve mankind.

Five thousands years ago or more kingship was lowered from heaven to earth. This was as a result of the Anunnaki not wishing to bother with the day-to-day squabbling of man.

Enlil (the first God of Earth according to Sumerian texts) selected the kings who were to rule over Mankind, not as sovereigns but as servants of the God entrusted with the administration of divine laws of justice. Accordingly, Sumerian, Akkadian, and Babylonian kings opened their inscriptions of self-adoration by describing how Enlil had called them to Kingship. It is this Kingship that Sir Laurence Gardner refers to as the "Bloodline of the Holy Grail." These 'calls' issued by Enlil on behalf of himself and his father Anu—granted legitimacy to the ruler and outlined his functions. Even Hammurabi, who acknowledged a God named Marduk as the national God of Babylon, prefaced his code of laws by stating "Anu and Enlil named me to promote the welfare of the people … to cause justice to prevail in the land."

There came a time, before the great deluge, that the Earth was beginning to be overcrowded with mankind. By the third millennium BCE the Nephilim were declining in numbers and the children and grandchildren of Man, to say nothing of humans of divine parentage were crowding the great olden Gods for living space.

The Nephilim, we are told, reached the conclusion that they needed an intermediary between themselves and the masses of humans. They were, they decided, to be Gods, elu in Akkadian, meaning "lofty ones."

After the Flood, the Nephilim held lengthy meetings to debate the future relationship between gods and man. As a result of these deliberations, the Nephilim created four distinct regions or zones. Mesopotamia, the Nile valley and Indus valley zones were to be settled by Man.

The fourth area was to be a forbidden zone to Man. It was to be Holy, which actually means dedicated or restricted. This area could not be trespassed by Man without the permission of the gods. This territory reminds one of tales and urban legends concerning Area 51 in Nevada. Guards in high towers oversaw the land and trespassers were often killed on sight by, 'awesome weapons' wielded by fierce guards.

As a bridge between themselves as lords and Mankind, they introduced 'kingship' on earth: appointing a human ruler who would assure Mankind's service to the gods and channel the teachings and laws of the Gods to the people. Kingship on earth was established as a sacred duty for both social and military duties. It was not truly governmental, although the kings were the designated guardians of the people. The king could be described as being a Shepherd and he carried a shepherd's staff to signify his office. This symbol of office of a crook or crosier was later adopted by the Catholic Church and used in ceremonies overseen by the bishops.

The king was also adorned with a crown or tiara of gold, which signified the great wisdom of Anu. A scepter was also part of the king's regalia.

Specifically a king was to administer his city, and so govern as his particular God decreed. The king was the last hope for his people to obtain justice. He was not only the Chief Justice but also the head of the Temple. By administering the city, the king was responsible for all public works, community building and restoration. A king's mandate could be explained as follows: interpret the will of the Anunnaki; act as the representation of the people to the Anunnaki; and administer the city.

Sumerian texts tell us that the very first human to be responsible for the temple was Adapa (Adam of the bible). He was referred as the High Priest and of the Royal Seed (bloodline). Indeed, Adapa was the model for earthly kingship, and as such was the first priest-king.

Both Sumerian and Akkadian texts state that the Nephilim, following the Great Deluge, returned the 'lordship' over the lands, and had Mankind first rebuild the antediluvian cities exactly where thy had originally been and as they had been planned: "Let the bricks of all the cities be laid on the dedicated places, let all the (bricks) rest on holy places." Eridu, then, was first to be rebuilt. The Nephilim then helped the people plan and build the first royal city, and they blessed it. "May the city be the next, the place where mankind shall repose. May the King be a Shepherd."

As time went on, the gods became overlords, each jealously guarding the territory, industry, or profession over which they had been given dominion. Human kings were the intermediaries between the gods and the growing and spreading humanity. The claims of ancient kings that they went to war, conquered new lands, or subjugated distant peoples "on the command of my God" should not be taken lightly. Text after text makes it clear that this was literally so. The gods retained the power of conducting foreign affairs, for these affairs involved other gods in other territories. Accordingly, they had the final say in matters of war or peace.

Sir Laurence Gardner, in his book *The Genesis of the Grail Kings*, stated that the monarchs of the Grail succession were called Messiahs (Anointed Ones) because, in the early days of Mesopotamia and Egypt, they were anointed with the fat of the sacred Messeh (the holy dragon or crocodile). By virtue of this, they were also called Dragons. The Dragon, emblematic of wisdom, was the epitome of the Holy Spirit, which, according to the Book of Genesis, moved upon the waters of time, while the Grail was the perpetual Blood Royal—the Sang Real. Originally, in old Mesopotamia, it was called the Gra-al—the Sacred Blood of the Dragon Queens, and it was said to be the "nectar of supreme excellence". The ancient Greeks called it ambrosia.

The Messianic succession of the Royal Bloodline, as previously stated was genetically created to serve mankind. The Anunnaki, from ancient Sumer, used their creation chamber to alter the DNA of Man. This majestic bloodline starting with Adam continued to King David and to Jesus through his mother Mary and is still present today.

The rule of kingly descent through the senior female line appears to have been established from the outset when a dispute over entitlement arose between the brothers Enki and Enlil. The Anunnaki overlords were said to have governed by way of a Grand Assembly of nine councilors who sat at Nippur. The nine consisted of eight members (seven males and a female), who held the Rings of divine justice, along with their president, Anu, who held the One Ring to bind them all. Not only does this conform with the nine kingdoms of the Volsunga Saga, which sites Odin (Wotan) as the ultimate presidential Ring Lord, but it is also commensurate with the seven archangels of Hebraic record along with their two supervisors, the Lord of the Spirits and the Most High (equivalent to Anu). As the original God-kings of Mesopotamia, this Assembly was said to have introduced kingly practice, which, according to the Sumerian King List was 'lowered from heaven.' Please also refer to Chapter VII, One Ring To Rule Them All.

The BBC World News Edition has published a story entitled, "Gilgamesh tomb believed found." The article is dated Tuesday 29 April 2003.

The article states that archaeologists in Iraq believe they may have found the lost tomb of King Gilgamesh, which is the subject of the oldest 'book' in history.

The Epic of Gilgamesh, written by a Middle Eastern scholar 2,500 years before the birth of Christ, commemorated the life of the ruler of the city of Uruk, from which Iraq gets its name.

"I don't want to say definitely it was the grave of King Gilgamesh, but it looks very similar to that described in the epic," Jorg Fassbinder, of the Bavarian department of Historical Monuments in Munich told the BBC World Service's Science in Action program.

Remember when the land was partitioned into four areas: three areas or zones were to be where Man dwells; and the fourth was to be a restricted area, a holy place. It was this holy place that Gilgamesh was trying to reach in his epic poem. He pleaded with the Gods to allow him entrance:

Let me enter the Land, let me raise my Shem …
By the life of my Goddess mother who bore me,
Of the pure faithful king, my father—
My step direct to the Land!

BOOK TWO

9

King Arthur and Glastonbury

Seaview of Tintagel.

Atlantic Ocean breakers crash against the cliffs and gale force winds buffet the outcrop of rock that characterizes Tintagel Head. In fact, the wind is so strong that when you stand and look out to sea on the hill above the ruins you are in real danger of being lifted into the air and thrown over the cliff. You would be thrown down one hundred meters to the churning, foaming water and jagged boulders below.

Man has inhabited this ancient fortress for over two thousand years. It is where the Arthur stone was found. This 6th century artifact is a broken piece of slate that was found during excavation the eastern terrace of Tintagel. The slate was inscribed with the name Artognov, which in Latin means the name Arthnou, and like Arthur is derived from the Celtic word arth, which means 'bear'. It is likely that the Arthur Stone was built into a wall of the building, where it remained buried for over 1400 years.

In the movie Excalibur, Tintagel was depicted as the castle where Merlin transformed Uther Pendragon into the likeness of Gorlois, the duke of Cornwall, who subsequently made love to his wife, the beautiful Queen Igraine. It was as a result of this union that Arthur was born nine months later.

In 2002, I accompanied my wife Carolyn to England to visit her parents and to do a little sightseeing. We had made plans to spend some time in Cornwall investigating King Arthur and his legend. The first stop on our quest was to visit Tintagel Castle, which some say was the original birthplace of Arthur, and the strongholds of the Earls of Cornwall.

Today, the town of Tintagel is accessible by car, bus or train. From the town you follow a road approximately one-half mile downhill to the ruins. Then it's all up hill from there. If you are a poor climber or have a heart condition I would not recommend this tour. The stairs are very steep and it is a long way up to the castle. I spent a couple of days scrambling up and down the ruins videotaping everything I could see. There are excellent historical guides that hold informal seminars on site and explain what life was like in the 6th Century and how the legend of King Arthur was associated with Cornwall.

The castle was originally connected to the mainland by a natural causeway. Sometime during the ensuing centuries this causeway collapsed and was replaced by a man-made bridge.

Tintagel is like no other castle in England. It consists of two sections: a steep headland connected originally by a natural, narrow, land bridge, to the island fortress, and sheer cliffs and dangerous rocks and shoals that guard the castle's approach. The ruins of the castle can be found in both sections.

Ancient stonewalls greeted invaders on every side and continued up the sides of the rock-face where even more impressive battlements were found. On the main or largest level we find the architectural outlines of buildings, including a great hall.

Tintagel rises even higher and another level shows the remains of more buildings and fortified stone emplacements. It is here that we find an opening in the earth. It consists of a tunnel that leads mysteriously down several levels. Unfortunately, this area is partitioned off and is out of bounds to tourists. I would definitely like to explore this tunnel.

Much of Tintagel was hidden in plain view until a fire broke out in the peat that makes up much of this mound. The fire burned so hot that the vegetation was totally destroyed. The outlines of previously undiscovered buildings peeked through the now barren soil.

Below Tintagel there are two caves, and only one cave, Merlin's cave, runs completely under Tintagel. You can only get to the pebble-strewn beach during low tide and enter the caves. I was lucky enough to walk through Merlin's cave twice. On my first, I used the traditional route of climbing down over a few boulders and walking along the beach for a few hundred yards to the cave. I entered the cave, which has a large opening and immediately heard the roar of the ocean coming through from the far end of the cave. I was in a small group exploring the cave. The light was fading so the tourists returned to the road above the beach. I was determined to come back and finish my exploration another day.

The view from inside Merlin's Cave.

The next day I wanted to visit the cave again but it was high tide and the beach was underwater. Not to be deterred I managed to climb over a fence and scramble down to the beach below, from where I made my way into Merlin's cave once again. I walked carefully over the rocks avoiding the water and examining the sides of the cave for signs of secret passages. The lighting was poor and may have contributed to the fact that I didn't find a trace of any secret openings. Tradition has it that there is a hidden door leading to Merlin's secret chamber somewhere in the interior of this huge rock. This visit was also shortened by the tide, which was rapidly cutting off my exit from the cave.

This once mighty fortress was abandoned because it simply cost too much to maintain. Natural erosion, by both wind and water, destroyed Tintagel Castle, an accomplishment no army ever claimed.

Our Arthurian quest led us to the town of Glastonbury, which is in Somerset, where legend tells us that Joseph of Arimathea, the Virgin Mary's uncle, built a place of worship called the 'Old Church', which later became known as the Lady or St. Mary's Chapel. We were visiting England during the month of May and it was approximately the middle of the month when we visited Glastonbury. It was truly a beautiful day; clouds were nowhere to be seen as the spring sun warmed us. Light jackets were necessary, but overall the weather was fantastic.

Inside the Abbey.

Glastonbury is also home to the famous Glastonbury Abbey. Originally built by a local Somerset man, this stone church forms the base of the west end of where the nave now stands. The Saxons, who had been converted to Christianity, conquered the ancient county of Somerset in the 7th Century. The Abbot of Glastonbury, St. Dunstan, who became the Archbishop of Canterbury in 960AD, enlarged this church in the 10th century. In 1066, the wealth of the Abbey could not save the Saxon monks from the invasion and subsequent conquest of England by the Normans.

Supposedly, Arthur was buried in the graveyard of Glastonbury Abbey south of the Lady Chapel, at a great depth, between two monumental pillars.

To protect the burial spot the monks allegedly excavated the spot. They dug down seven feet and unearthed a stone slab. Under this slab was a lead cross about a foot long, with a Latin inscription: "Hic iacet sepultus inclitus rex arturius in insula avalonia," which translates as "Here lies buried the renowned King Arthur in the Isle of Avalon."

All that was found below the cross were some small bones and a scrap of hair. The monks thought the hair, which crumbled away when touched, belonged to Guinevere.

The bones were interned into caskets and reburied in 1278. A black marble tomb marked the burial area, which was positioned before the high altar of the main Abbey church. There they remained until the Abbey was vandalized after the dissolution. No one has seen or heard of them since.

This plaque states that here is where King Arthur and Guinevere are buried.

Today, an engraved plaque indicates their original burial spot. This is located at the far end of the abbey directly opposite the entrance to the park. Portions of the buildings, including ancient archways, still tower high above the manicured lawns.

Glastonbury Abbey is huge. The ruins of the abbey and surrounding parkland include 36 acres, which include a fishpond, a duck pond and a cider orchard. The abbey is situated at the foot of Glastonbury Tor, which means mound or hill.

A short walk from the Abbey along High Street is St John's Anglican Church. St. John's is home to an invaluable stained glass window, which ironically is of Joseph of Arimathea. I really wanted to see the stained glass; so, my wife and I walked up to the church. It was closed and was only open for services. Not much of a tourist attraction. The gates were not locked so we walked around the property. I think I saw the window from the outside of the church, although in truth it could have been anything because the interior of the church was not illuminated.

The church is also famous for the thorn that still grows there. Its botanical name is Crataegus oxyacantha and it is of the Levantine variety of hawthorn or applewort. It comes from the Near East and only grows in Glastonbury. Legend has it that when Joseph was transporting the Holy Grail he accidentally struck his thorn staff into the ground and it immediately sprouted into a living bush. Today, the bush grows in at least three religious sites: St. John's, on the Abbey grounds, and on the upper slopes of Wearyall Hill. This thorn flowers around January 5th and its blossoms are sent to the reigning king or queen of England.

Glastonbury has a handy and affordable bus tour of the area, which picks you up from the parking area and transports you to the foot of the Tor. Here you can climb a set of stairs with handrails all the way to the top. Don't panic there are rest areas along the way. I admit it; I stopped a few times to catch my breath. A five hundred feet climb is not a pleasant walk in the park.

The long walk to the top of Glastonbury Tor.

Around the sides of the Tor is an intricate, some say mystical system of terracing. This man-made hill once consisted of a maze that worshippers had to solve in order to reach the top of the Tor. Although weathered and eroded, but still well defined, it has been interpreted as following an ancient magical pattern. If the maze on the Tor is real, human labor formed it four or five thousand years ago. This was the same time period that saw the creation of other such earthworks such as Stonehenge, and the building of the Egyptian pyramids.

The tower of the church of St. Michael crowns the Tor. Built on the top of the Tor the church is named after the Archangel Michael, the warrior Saint who is remembered for defeating the powers of darkness. This church consists of a solitary tower that remains in remarkably good condition and is a great meeting place for tourists who choose to linger and study the stonework rather than brave the wind and the sun.

St. Michael's Church sits on top of Glastonbury Tor.

The top of the Tor is an excellent place to lie down on the grass, next to the earth, and dream of what was or of what may have been. Was King Arthur buried in the Abbey? Is this area of Somerset really Avalon? Did Jesus and Joseph of Arimathea really visit here and build a Christian church? Was the Holy Grail really a cup and is it buried nearby? All of these questions and more flooded my mind so I choose instead to dream of Merlin.

We descended the hill by following a long path that gradually delivered us back to Bush Combe and Dod Lane. These streets led back into the town and to the car park.

I saw a documentary movie on the Glastonbury area in 2004, and with the aid of computer generated graphics (CGI) one could see how this entire area was surrounded by water. The show basically hypothesized that some two thousand years ago, the sea washed right up to the foot of the Tor, nearly encircling the cluster of hills. The sea gradually receded and was replaced by a vast lake leaving an isolated island towering above the waves. An old name for this island was taken from the Celtic legend and that name was Avalon. Avalon was said to be an isle of enchantment.

Ancient myth has it that Avalon was a meeting place for the dying: a portal where the dead would pass over to another level of existence. It was here that the mortally wounded Arthur came to be ferried across the water to Avalon. This was the home of the Lord of the Underworld and a place where fairy folk lived.

What a wondrous spot. Glastonbury is home to the Arthurian legend, the founding of the Christian Church in England, and the home of fairy folk. It is a place where myths converge and quests are born.

Writers note: J.R.R. Tolkien worked on and published a prose translation of Sir Gawain and Green Knight along with E.V. Gordon for Oxford University Press, 1936. We can only speculate as to what influence the Sir Gawain and Green Knight had on *The Lord of the Rings.*

10

One Ring to Rule Them All

One Ring to rule them all,
One Ring to find them,
One Ring to bring them all
and in the darkness bind them.

The above quote is very familiar to everyone who has either seen any of the three movies, or has read Tolkien's ring trilogy. The one ring binds all the other rings to the Dark Lord Sauron, who as Gandalf cautioned Frodo, "The rumors that you have heard are true: he has indeed arisen again and left his hold in Mirkwood and returned to his ancient fortress in the Dark Tower of Mordor."

Where did Tolkien get the original idea for the rings in his saga? Did he have a dream about the rings, did he have a true inspiration or a deeply religious epiphany, or was there some other source?

Remember that Tolkien's daytime job was as an Oxford University professor of Anglo-Saxon and English language. As such, he was aware of ancient myths, especially the tales of the North featuring the Norse God Odin, King of the Vikings. Odin is the same God as the Saxon's God Wotan. Odin was a Ring-Lord and governed as president over nine kingdoms. Each ruler of the individual kingdoms was given a ring from Odin, and note that it was Odin's ring that bound all of the other rings and their wearers to him.

Tolkien was so taken by the myths of the North that he learned to read Finnish perfectly, in order to understand the history and myth of Finland in their original language. Titles of some of Finnish myths seem familiar, including The Saga of the Ring and The Kingdom of the Circle.

When Tolkien was asked about his setting for Middle-earth, he stated that he believed the historical period of the story to be approximately 4000 BCE. He added, "The pot of soup (the caldron of the story) has always been boiling and to it have continually been added new bits."

Geographically, Tolkien suggested, that Middle-earth's homeland was to be found in the Nordic countries, especially Finland. Later, we will explore this Norse myth known as the Volsunga Saga and the composer Wagner's The Ring of the Nibelungs and see how they relate, inspire and mirror *The Lord of the Rings*.

If we look back in history for evidence of the ring's origin we must once again transport 6000 years to ancient Sumer, and rely on the lost, now found and finally translated clay tablets and copper cylinders of the God-Kings. These were the original God-Kings of Mesopotamia who kingly power was given them from heaven. Once translated, this pictorial history of the Anunnaki overlords, demonstrated that they ruled their earthly kingdoms through the creation of a Grand Assembly (parliament). This Grand Assembly was consisted of eight councilors: one for each kingdom or region. The eight members included seven males and one female. They were given and ruled by their rings, which were reported to be of divine power. It was Ring power that was responsible for the establishment of municipal government and kingly rule.

The president of the Grand Assembly held the One Ring that bound the member councilors to the president.

This knowledge of ancient history is communicated centuries, millennia later, by means of oral and written folk tales and myths. Are we all simply receptacles of genetic memory, and now remembering vicariously our forgotten heritage, through Tolkien's finally detailed characters transposed to the big screen or within the printed word.

The oldest ring tale is Icelandic, based on Norse mythology and called The Volsunga Saga. It combines over forty tales from the North and is told by William Morris. The text of this edition is based on that published as *The Story of the Volsungs*, translated by William Morris and Eirik Magnusson.

The following is an overview of his translation. It features the God Odin, who as previously mentioned is the ruler of the Kingdom of the Nine Worlds. Interestedly, part of the story occurs in the forest of Mirkwood. Tolkien states that Sauron arose from the dark forest of Mirkwood.

The story relates how Prince Sigmund of the Volsung dynasty, like King Arthur, pulls the great sword of Odin from a tree, in which the God had driven the sword up to its hilt. Arthur pulls Excalibur from a rock.

The tales revolve around Prince Sigmund's son Sigurd, who inherits the magical sword of Odin and defeats a dragon that guards the treasure of the Dwarf Lord Andarvi. Andarvi is a water-dwarf who has a magical ring made of red gold.

The magical ring enables its master to weave great wealth. Like all magical rings, this ring also had a curse.

Sigurd then travels to the land of the Franks where he encounters a tower which houses a beautiful maiden named Brynhild, who is a Valkyrie battle-maiden of Odin. She once carried the souls of heroes to the land of the dead—Valhalla. This could well be the genesis of the Rapunzel fairy tale.

Brynhild is in a deep sleep, apparently the victim of a poison pinprick from a sleep-thorn. She is imprisoned in a tower surrounded by a ring of fire. This part of the tale could well be the origin of Sleeping Beauty whose deep sleep was as a result of eating a poisoned apple.

The prince awakens Brynhild and they fall in love and become lovers. Sigurd, as a sign of his love, places the Ring on Brynhild's finger and she falls asleep again, bound to him forever.

Sigurd rides to the Rhineland of the Nibelung, where he is drugged and loses his memory. He then meets and marries Princess Gudrun, but eventually the power of the Ring emerges and he recovers his memory and returns to Brynhild.

In the meantime, Brynhild learns that Sigurd has married and swears revenge. She knew nothing of the magic potion that Sigurd drank which caused the memory loss. As a result Sigurd is murdered and Brynhild finally learns the details of the memory loss and the marriage. Her combined guilt and lost love causes her to commit suicide.

Princess Gudrun, who in her grief weighs down her apron with rocks and leaps from a cliff into the sea, then recovers the magical ring. She is still wearing the magical ring on her finger and thus completes the Ring Cycle by returning the ring to the water as it was originally owned by the water-dwarf.

A contemporary tale to the Volsunga Saga is The Nibelungenlied. Written about 800 years ago, it was told in Burgundy France and featured Siegfried as the hero of this gothic tale.

The Nibelungenlied is a German epic poem which was written sometime around 1200, probably in what is today Austria. The title means Song of the Nibelungs. Nibelungen is the plural of "Nibelung," which refers to a dynasty, which is conquered by the hero or protagonist of the epic, the dragon-slayer Siegfried. The word "lied" means "lay," which is a Germanic word for a song, poem, or lyric. The poem exists in more than thirty manuscripts, but three main versions represent the story, as we know it. For the purposes of study, many modern editions are translated in prose rather than rhymed poetic form to be more accessible to students.

Reasons why the Nibelungenlied has enjoyed such a wide readership for so many centuries include: much is known about the historical context of the poem as well as about the literary sources it drew on, including mythology and legend. The story is one of heroes, romance, courtly manners, deception, and revenge. Many readers for its literary techniques and for its adventurous qualities and complex characters have enjoyed it as well.

The Nibelungenlied combines elements of many different historical, legendary, and mythological tales. The legend of the Nibelungs arose from the historical destruction of the Burgundian kingdom on the Rhine River by Etzel's army of Huns (later identified in legend with the army of Attila the Hun) around the year 437. Many other characters in the Nibelungenlied have some historical basis as well. Gunther was King of Burgundy, and Dietrich is thought to be based on Theodoric the Ostrogoth, who was King of Italy in 493. The events in the poem, however, were altered and combined with other legends when the story was first written down for a medieval audience around 1200.

The Nibelungenlied and the legends it was based on existed in oral form long before it was ever written down. A version of the Nibelungenlied was first translated into modern German in 1757 under the title of Kriemhild's Revenge. Many more versions followed, but no English translation appeared until 1814. The first complete English prose version appeared in 1848. There have been many more, in both prose as well as verse form.

The Nibelungenlied, as an epic, celebrates the achievements, adventures, and battles of several heroic figures. It also encompasses elements of the romance genre as well, including tales of knights, courtly behavior, and chivalry. The Nibelungenlied draws on history, mythology, and legend for its details. It encompasses themes such as heroism, feudalism, justice and revenge, honor, loyalty, deception, dreams, and the importance of "keeping up appearances."

The 'meaning' of the Nibelungenlied is difficult to determine. It does not have a clearly defined moral message for the reader. However, it raises important questions about the nature of loyalty, honor, and what constitutes tragedy. It also attracts study and commentary purely on the basis of its accomplished literary features, such as its structure, character development, and the use of foreshadowing. The Nibelungenlied poet combined disparate material and stories into a comprehensive whole that captures modern readers no less than audiences of eight hundred years ago.

As mentioned earlier, J.R.R. Tolkien was not the only person to write about a primordial time featuring wizards, battles and rings of power. Richard Wagner, the famous 19th Century composer, wrote his famous opera "The Ring of the Nibelungs" and it is presented in three parts (a trilogy), plus an introduction.

Some speculate that both Tolkien and Wagner were inspired by an ancient Norse tale entitled the Legend of the Nibelungenlied, which literally translates as The Song of the Dwarves.

Wagner's saga centers around the Norse God Wotan (Odin), who rules by the laws engraved on his spear. He wants a new fortress and hires two giants to build the fabled Valhalla. He steals the treasure of the Niebelung dwarf Alberich to pay the giants. Alberich gained his fortune after he forged a magic ring from gold he stole from the Rhinemaidens (mermaids). Wotan realizes the ring gives the bearer mastery of the world, but is bound to give it to the giants.

Tolkien, when *The Lord of the Rings* was compared to Wagner's *The Ring of the Nibelungs*, stated that the only similarity between the two stories was that "Both rings are round."

The idea of the importance or magic of a ring or circle was universally accepted, especially in the British Isles. Ancients celebrated this belief by creating circles of earth, wood and stone. The largest and most famous is Stonehenge. No one today knows why the monoliths were erected, though many postulate that the stones have astronomical significance.

In 1990 the British Tourism Board hired our company to write a story about Torbay, one of their most important and largest tourist areas. They referred to it as the heart of the English Riviera. Situated in southwest England, it comprises three towns: Brixham, Paignton, and Torquay.

I will always remember this trip because I toured Torbay and related tourist areas in the middle of the winter. Ironically, I was there to write about sun, sand and surf, and was plummeted by gale force winds and crashing waves whose spray towered 50 feet into the air and soaked everything and everyone nearby.

This was my first trip to England and one of the great things I had arranged prior to the trip was a Brit Railway pass. This allowed me to travel anywhere in the country by train.

The local British Tourism representative met me at my hotel and took me to all the local tourist attractions where I was able to photograph the scenery and interview individuals to provide background and color to the piece.

One of my favorite memories was of seeing a reproduction of Sir Francis' ship the Golden Hind. Unimaginably small was my first impression. It looked no larger than 50 feet long and 20 feet wide. And this was the pride of the English navy and the scourge of the Spanish Armada of 1558.

Later I visited Torre Abbey, Torquay's most historic building. The Abbey is set on a splendid piece of land with beautiful gardens, manicured green lawns with scattered trees, and a tropical palm house. Behind the Abbey is a barn known as the 'Tithe Barn'. It is one of Britain's most complete medieval barns. In 1588 the barn was used to house 400 Spanish prisoners from the Spanish Armada, and so it is rightly named 'The Spanish Barn'. This is where many prisoners died of dreadful disease and willful neglect.

When I had finished my story, I took a serendipitous train trip back to London and stopped in Salisbury to visit the famous Abbey and experience Stonehenge firsthand.

I took a local bus to Salisbury Plain on which Stonehenge is built.

Some of the anticipated enchantment of Stonehenge was lost when our bus pulled into the parking lot; we walked through an underground tunnel before emerging to a procession of souvenir and concession stands. Ignoring the mundane, I followed the path to one of my heart's greatest fantasies … standing in the presence of gigantic monoliths, thousands of years old, possibly of great religious and astronomical importance.

This ancient circle, which some claim has druidic roots, is today roped off from the public. I yearned to caress the polished stones and absorb their ancient secrets through my fingertips. This was a travesty; it was like showing a thirsty man a cool sparkling brook and forbidding him to drink. I should have jumped the ropes and entered the enchanted realm protected by the circle. It may be a portal to magical places or the wellspring of ancient knowledge, but I didn't.

Instead, I thought I would observe the majesty of this collection of upright and toppled stones from where I stood. I tried to envision energy emissions radiating from the monoliths, like the patterns formed by metal filings displaying magnetic fields. I strained to see King Arthur or Merlin in the circle but all I saw was untrammeled grass and undisturbed earth through the forbidding ropes.

It was February and I was standing on a plain exposed to all of nature's elements and instead of experiencing mystic vibrations, all I felt was the sting of a cold wind. The concession stands and the walk-through tunnel were no longer mundane but a sought after haven.

Many believe that Stonehenge is unique, but the British Isles has many examples of stone circles. During my 2002 trip to England I visited one other, but less known stone circle. My wife's parents live in Bedfordshire, England, which is about 60 miles north of London. We took several trips from Bedford and one of the first was to the Rollright Stones. These stones also form a circle but the highest stone is only about 5 feet tall. It is said that it is impossible to accurately count the stones because the number changes on every count. I asked my wife and her brother Nick to join me in counting the stones and we all came up with a different total! Unlike Stonehenge, this stone circle has a legend surrounding its creation.

An ambitious King with the goal of conquering all of England led his army as far as the Rollrights. Here he met a witch. Her name was Mother Shipton of Shipton-under-Wychwood and she lived between 1488-1551. She challenged the King with these words, "Seven long strides shalt thou take And if Long Compton thou canst see, King of England thou shalt be."

Off went the King, shouting, "Stick, stock, stone As King of England I shall be known."

On his seventh stride the ground rose up before him in a long mound sometimes known as the Arch-Druid's barrow. The witch laughed and declared, "As Long Compton thou canst not see King of England thou shalt not be. Rise up stick and stand still stone For King of England thou shalt be none; Thou and thy men hoar stones shall be And I myself an eldern tree."

And so it was that the King became the King Stone, his men the King's Men Stone Circle, and his treacherous and conniving knights the 'Whispering Knights,' although some say that the knights were actually at prayer.

Legend has it that one day the spell will be broken and that the King and his men will return to life and continues their conquest of England. (source: http://www.rollrightstones.co.uk/history1.shtml)

Circles from mythology, nature and ancient history surrounded Tolkien and were important elements of his life. These circles formed the rings or links of a chain that connected and held tight Tolkien's real world and those of his imagination.

11

The Eye of Power

The All Seeing Eye of the U.S. Great Seal.

When Frodo and Sam were in the city of Galadhrim, the Lady Galadriel, an Elf-Queen, took them toward the southern slopes of the hill of Caras Galadhon, through a high green hedge and into an enclosed garden. The hobbits followed the tall, white, and fair Lady down many steps to the bottom where they found on a low pedestal carved like "a branching tree ... a basin of silver, wide and shallow, and beside it stood a silver ewer."

"Here is the Mirror of Galadriel," she said, "I have brought you here so that you make look in it, if you will."

Frodo stared into the pool of dark water. He saw mountains; he thought he saw Gandalf, and Bilbo walking ceaselessly about his room, papers everywhere. He thought he saw the sea roar up into a great storm. He saw a ship with black sails and a city with a white tree, and then the water in the mirror turned black again. Out of the blackness an 'Eye' was forming and it grew until it made up almost the entire mirror. Frodo's fear of the 'Eye' was so great that he could not move, could not yell out and could not change his gaze. "The Eye was rimmed with fire, but was itself glazed, yellow as a cat's, watchful and intent, and the black slit of its pupil opened on a pit, a window into nothing." Then the vision really got scary when, "the Eye began to rove, searching this way and that; and Frodo knew with certainty and horror that among the many things that it sought he himself was one."

Although Frodo and Sam had really just started on their journey, it was clear that Sauron's Eye would be a constant yet mostly unseen companion on their quest. Many miles later and almost totally exhausted, their food running out, the duo approached Mount Doom, "the mantling clouds swirled and for a mount drew aside; and then he saw, rising black, blacker and darker than the vast shades amid which it stood, the cruel pinnacles and iron crown of the topmost tower of Barad-dur. One moment it stared out, but as from some great window immeasurably high there stabbed northward a flame of red, the flicker of a piercing Eye; and then the shadows were furled again and the terrible vision was removed."

In fact with every step towards the gates of Mordor, Frodo felt the Ring on its chain about his neck grow more burdensome. He was now beginning to feel it as an actual weight dragging him earthwards. Far more the Eye troubled him: so he called it to himself. It was that more than the drag of the Ring that made him cower and stoop as he walked. The Eye: that horrible growing sense of a hostile will that strove with great power to pierce all shadows of cloud, and earth, and flesh, and to see you: to pin you under its deadly gaze, naked immovable. So thin, so frail and thin, the veils were become that still warded it off. Frodo knew just where the present habitation and heart of that will not was: as certainly as a man can tell the direction of the sun with his eyes shut. He was facing it, and its potency beat upon his brow....

The Eye of Sauron is an extension of his evil and is a constant reminder of dread for Frodo. It was as if the very stare from the eye seemed to sap Frodo of his strength and his will to continue on toward Mount Doom. Sauron's 'all seeing eye' was similar to a reptile or a snake. Could this characteristic of the eye be related to the amphibious Nummo race?

Even the Anunnaki had a version of Tolkien's 'Eye of Sauron': it was known as the 'Terrible Eye.' The Anunnaki were thought to possess supernatural machines that made it possible for Gods to communicate with other Gods in Heaven. Temples at Lagast, Ur and Mari housed sacred objects called 'eye idols.' One of the greatest examples of the "eye idols" was found at Tell Brak in northwestern Mesopotamia. This temple is decorated with hundreds of eye symbols and features an altar on which a huge double-eye symbol was displayed. According to Zecharia Sitchin this double eye symbol is, most likely, a simulation of the Anunnaki's original 'Terrible Eye.'

Enlil, son of Anu, possessed the "bond heaven-earth," and from his "awesome city Nippur" he could "raise the beams that search the heart of all the lands"—"even that could scan all the lands."

Ninuta the Sumero-Babylonian God of rain, fertility, war, thunderstorms, wells, canals, floods, the plough, and the South Wind, was said that he had a terrible eye and that, "His raised Eye scans the land" and that "His raised Beam searches the land."

The Anunnaki had many examples of supernatural equipment. One of the greatest communication devices could well be the Ark of the Covenant. This communication tool was electrically operated and was portable enough to be carried from place to place. Inserting two long wooden poles between four golden rings could only carry the Ark of the Covenant. By touching the sides of the Ark with anything other than by wooden poles brought instant death.

Certainly we don't have to go back to ancient Sumerian or Babylon to find evidence of the terrible eye or the 'all seeing eye.' All United States citizens or holders of U.S. currency realize, almost immediately, that U.S. currency pictures the Great Seal on the back of the U.S. Dollar Bill. It is this Great Seal that includes the pyramid that we are all familiar with and near the top of the pyramid is where the 'All Seeing Eye' or the 'Eye in the Pyramid' is found.

The 'Eye of Providence', sometimes referred to in Masonic ritual as the 'All-Seeing Eye' (of a Deity) is found in the ritual of most jurisdictions, reminding a Mason that the Supreme Architect of the Universe is judging his words and deeds. The pyramid appears in the ritual of some jurisdictions and represents the great builders of the past. However, their combined usage is essentially non-existent except by a few fanciful representations done by individuals whose imagination has soared beyond that of the black text ritual.

If the Masonic conspiracy isn't bad enough, the government has a plan to establish an all-seeing, omnipresent set of eyes in the sky to keep an unblinking view of the entire world at once. Representatives from the military, spy agencies, and the defense industry met recently in New Orleans on Oct. 17, 2003, to find ways to put a new generation of spy satellites in orbit to aid in war, homeland security, and spy craft. But talking about the Big Brother vision in a hotel ballroom is proving to be a whole lot easier than executing it in orbit. Several of the satellite systems are wrapped in controversy, cost overruns or long delays.

"We need to know something about everything all the time," said Stephen Cambone, undersecretary of defense for intelligence. Speaking to the gathering of nearly 1,400 at the Geo-Intel 2003 conference here at the French Quarter's edge, he added, "We need an illuminator, throwing into relief all the pictures and activities on the Earth's surface. And then we need to be able to switch on the spotlight, or alert other systems, to dive deep."

"This system has to be never-blinking, never-straying," added Rich Haver, a Northrop Grumman executive, and Defense Secretary Donald Rumsfeld's former special assistant for intelligence. "Our enemies can never be sure when they're being looked at."

Speaking of enemies, the next chapter narrates the first war that featured both gods and men.

12

The First Battle of Gods and Men

Tolkien was thoughtful enough to give us a breakdown of Sauron's mighty army. Of Sauron and the war Gandalf stated, "Other evils there may come; for Sauron is himself but a servant or emissary."

Sauron's forces did not consist merely of the Nazul, who were also called Ring-wraiths and were the slaves of the nine rings of men the chief servants of Sauron, but also orcs and the trolls, and even humans. We can only imagine what riches and rewards were promised by Sauron to these people to betray mankind itself. The enemy consisted of Easterlings with axes, and Variags of Khard, Southrons in scarlet, and out of Far Harda black men like half-trolls with eyes and red tongues.

The Lieutenant of the Tower of Barad-dur, who was a human himself, led Sauron's army onto the battlefield. It was said that he had no name. He was a renegade who came from a race named the Black Numernoreans. They worshipped Sauron, and it was said he was crueler than the orcs. So, Tolkien portrays an army of diverse peoples. Some are human, some subhuman, some are gods, some are demigods, some are good, and some are definitely evil. The first battle of men and gods was no less important for the peoples of Egypt as it was for the peoples of Middle-earth.

This first battle involving men, fighting side by side, with gods, began in Upper Egypt in the year 363. The calendar was calculated based on the number of years a god or pharaoh reigned. Therefore, the first year of a ruler was year one, followed by year two and so on.

Ra stood staring out over the sea of dunes, stretching past the horizon. The north prevailing winds were strong this time of year and carried coarse sand that stung his face. Ra, the Holy One, the Falcon of the Horizon, was waiting patiently for his nephew, Horus, to arrive. He knew that an unknown enemy was planning to attack his kingdom, and he needed Horus to help defeat the invader. Ra and his troops had traveled to Horus' city-state Uauaatet, which was in the land of Khenn (Egypt). They had traveled in Ra's boat, which was said to have flown to the Throne Place of Horus. Ra's boat was also called celestial because it could ascend to the highest heavens.

Tolkien stated that the only similarity between *The Ring of the Nibelungs* and *The Lord of the Rings* was that "Both rings are round." We beg to differ and the following similarities are offered for comparison purposes only:

Legend: The Ring of the Nibelungs—ROFN The Lord of the Rings—LOTR

In ROFN Alberich forges a Ring of Power.	In LOTR Sauron forges a Ring of Power.
In the ROFN Wotan needs the giants to build Valhalla.	In the LOTR the Elves need Sauron to forge their Rings of Power.
In the ROFN the Ring gives the bearer world domination.	In the LOTR the Ring gives the bearer world domination.
In the ROFN the Ring is cursed and betrays its bearer.	In the LOTR the Ring is evil and betrays its bearer.
In the ROFN Fafner (one of the giants hired to build Valhalla) kills his brother Fasolt to get the Ring.	In the LOTR Sméagol strangles his friend Deagol for the Ring.
In the ROFN, Fafner hides in a cave for centuries.	In the LOTR Sméagol-Gollum hides in a cave for centuries.
In the ROFN Siegfried (son of Wotan) inherits the shards of his father's sword.	In the LOTR Aragorn inherits the shards of his father's sword.
In the ROFN the Ring gives the bearer world domination.	In the LOTR the Ring gives the bearer world domination.
In the ROFN Brunnhide, one of the famous Valkyrie, who wears armor with breastplates and a helmet with horns, gives up her immortality for Siegfried.	In the LOTR Arwen, an Elf princess, gives up her immortality to marry Aragorn.
In the ROFN Wotan plays "riddles" for the life of Mime (he is the brother of the dwarf Alberich).	In the Hobbit Gollum plays "riddles" for the life of Bilbo, when he is lost and separated from his friends.
In the ROFN a dragon guards the entrance to the Niebelung dwarf Alberich's cave of gold.	In the LOTR a dragon guards the dwarves' hoard.

In the ROFN the Gods renounce the world and await the end.	In the LOTR the Elves renounce the world and prepare to leave Middle-earth.
In the ROFN the Ring is retuned it its place of origin, the River Rhine.	In the LOTR the Ring is returned to its place of origin, Mount Doom.
In the ROFN Hagen murders Siegfried to steal the ring but is dragged to his death by the Rhinemaidens and falls into the river.	In the LOTR, Gollum falls into the volcano in Mount Doom.
In the ROFN the immortals are consumed by fire when Valhalla burns.	In the LOTR the immortals (Elves) leave middle-earth in their gray ships.
In the ROFN a new era emerges in the world.	In the LOTR a new era emerges in the world as the "time of man" arrives.
In the ROFN Siegfried has his father's sword re-forged.	In the LOTR Aragorn has his ancestor's sword re-forged.
In the ROFN Wotan is an old man who carries a spear.	In the LOTR Gandalf is an old wizard who carries a magical staff.

Horus, The Winged Measurer, when informed of his grandfather's arrival rushed to Ra's boat and bowed in his presence, saying, "O Falcon of the Horizon, I have seen the enemy conspire against thy Lordship, to take the Luminous Grown upon themselves."

Ra's spies had already given him this information. The big question in Ra's mind was who would dare to attack him and why. Both Ra and Horus were gods; a god or gods could only defeat them. Therefore they realized that the enemy was of divine parentage.

Ra instructed Horus to take his boat and locate the enemy. Ra's winged disk has become emblematic with him, and is found in many ancient cultures around the world today. The winged sun disk is one of the oldest religious symbols on earth.

Artist's conception of the God's Flying Boat.

Horus had the winged disk lift from the ground and rise to heaven. The craft banked to the side, accelerated and then leveled out thousands of feet above the shifting sand dunes. Far below, a serpentine cloud of dust was rising in the air, betraying a line of war chariots swiftly zigzagging in and out of drifts, following makeshift trails. The enemy forces had been spotted near what today is the city of Aswan.

Horus ordered that the ship's weapons to be made ready. These weapons hurled thunderbolts of lightning or electricity. They killed instantly and were both silent and invisible. These weapons, probably lasers, unleashed a 'storm' upon the enemy.

The 'storm' from the winged disk caused such devastation that the enemy was utterly destroyed and it was said that not a single creature was left alive. For this great achievement Horus gained the new name of "Great God, lord of heaven."

The Egyptians consider Horus their God of war, first as a son of Ra, then changing to become the son of Osiris. He was the protector and guide to the pharaoh and later pharaohs were believed to be his representative on earth. Horus was also the patron of young men, and the ideal of the dutiful son who grows up to become a just man.

Horus returned the winged disk to a terrestrial boat of Ra. When the flying disk landed, it rained and sparked a rainbow of brilliant colors that caused great anxiety among the people and their children.

Other retreating soldiers had been captured and were tethered tightly laying baking on the sand. Ra and his Goddess Ashtoreth watched their enemy struggle helplessly as their craft sailed by. Ra then had the captives brought to the outside of the city and then executed.

Horus, in anticipation of an invasion, had built a divine metal foundry, where unique weapons made of 'divine iron' were forged. Near this foundry, Horus, also had the first human army trained. They were called mesniu, which translates as the 'Metal People.'

The mesniu were, according to Egyptian traditions, the first men ever to have been armed by the gods with weapons made of metal. They also were, as we shall see the first men to have been enlisted by a god to fight in the wars between the gods.

Ra and Horus moved their armies north toward the heartland of Egypt, where he initially fought 'the enemies.' He was victorious in battle after battle, and other gods and goddesses, such as Istar, enlisted in Horus' cause.

Ra requested that Horus, scout the land northward, but Horus could not find 'the enemies.' It was then that Ra and other gods entered their vessel (a Winged Disk) and flew north to the waters there and entered them. Ra's vessel was also amphibious. The enemy could not be found on land, so Ra believed he could find their whereabouts in or near the water.

Horus didn't have a vessel like Ra's, so he was given a boat to sail upon the water.

The enemies were aware that Ra, Horus, and their armies were in the water and made themselves as crocodiles and hippopotami and attacked Ra's vessel.

It was then, for the first time that Horus called for his army of 'Metal People,' each armed with 'divine iron,' and they fought off the crocodiles and hippopotami. The 'Metal People' were so successful that they captured 651 of the enemy. Horus had them executed immediately.

Ra and Horus' armies again moved north following two fleeing enemy armies. Again, Horus, with his human army was victorious. It was at this time that the first aerial battles occurred. Once again Ra and Horus were successful and the land and waters were secured from Thebes to Dendera, and the way to the heartland of Egypt was open. They continued to advance northward and Horus ordered the 'Metal People' to guard their flanks. The enemy was being driven back and continued to retreat until they stopped on the shores of the Mediterranean Sea.

Horus, followed in the boat of Ra, armed with the 'divine iron,' and supported by the army of men. He searched for the enemy for four days and four nights without success. Ra then advised Horus to take the Winged Disk into the sky and search for the enemy. Horus complied and flew north again and this time found the retreating enemy. He threw his 'Divine Lance' (a missile) at the enemy and they were destroyed.

Still, remnants of the enemy did manage to escape by sailing back across the Mediterranean to the land of Seth. Finally, Ra and Horus knew the god Seth commanded the enemy they had been fighting.

In early times Seth was worshipped as the god of wind and the desert storms, and warriors prayed to him so that they would be granted the strength of the desert storms. Although he was thought of as being a dark and moody god, he was believed to be the ally of his brother and sister, Osiris and Isis, the counterpart to his sister-wife Nephthys, and the defender of their father, Ra.

With the entire enemy gone from Egypt, Horus and the army of 'Metal People' and Ra and his warriors advanced to the southern shores of the Mediterranean, where they regrouped and waited. For a time there was peace.

Seth also regrouped and rebuilt his army. When they were ready he ordered them once again to cross the waters and attack northern Egypt. A ferocious battle ensued but the outcome was the same. Seth's army was vanquished.

Ra and Horus, seizing the opportunity, crossed with their armies to the land of Seth to confront Seth once and for all. Seth, seeing the approaching armies, was so angry that he challenged Horus to a series of god versus god battles. These combats were fought in the air and on the ground.

Horus, with the help of 'Divine Iron' defeated Seth and the battle for Egypt was over.

Looking back upon this war, it is debatable if Ra and Horus, without the 'Divine Iron'and his army of 'Metal People' could have defeated Seth's army, battle after battle. Little is known of the might of Seth's army, but it is conceivable that its size equaled if not outnumbered those of Horus.

As a result of the contribution made by man in helping Horus win the war against Seth, he decreed that his human army "shall dwell in sanctuaries," and that they shall be rewarded with food and drink. As a direct result of these battles, man was elevated to serve as human aides and emissaries to the gods. Man attained the title Shamsu-Hor, which means "attendants of Horus."

Egyptians also note, that as a result of being trained as soldiers, man for the first time learned to raise his sword against other men.

In 1848 while excavating the entrance to the Seti Temple in Abydos, Egypt, Archeologists discovered strange wall coverings that were ten meters high and displayed images of unimaginable machines.

The engravings were thought to be over 3000 years old and have been the subject of debate since their discovery. It was not until the 20th century that the Arab newspaper Al-Sharq Al-Awsat published several photos taken in the Amon

Ra Temple in Karnak. The photos depicted a battle helicopter with a distinct rotor and a tail unit as well as modern jet fighters and strategic bombers.

The 19th century archeologists could not understand what they were seeing at the Seti Temple, but modern man could understand the machines and wonder aloud how and why they were engraved on a temple wall thousands of years ago. Pharaoh Seti I, to whom the Seti Temple was dedicated, was one of the most famous of the Egyptian pharaohs. His military feats were depicted on temples throughout Egypt and he was known as a conqueror that expanded the lands of the kingdom.

Do the engraved images of helicopters and airplanes support that fact that the Egyptians actually used flying vehicles to fight their enemies?

A respected Egyptologist Alan Alford went to Egypt to study the Abydos mystery. After researching the mysterious hieroglyphs, he told journalists that he believed that the engravings depicted a real helicopter as if it had been engraved by studying a model. Detractors and other Egyptologists claim that Seti I was also know as the 'Bee' and that the depictions of aerial craft were actually just mystical depictions of the flying insect.

Could some of these engravings relate to Ra's 'winged disk?'

In the next chapter we will discover what role the gods played and how they manipulated man in one of the most famous wars in ancient history.

13

The Real Battle for Troy

When the beacon fires of Gondor were lit, the king, tall and proud cried aloud to summon men to arms in the aid of Gondor. One can only imagine the cry let out by King Menelaus when he returned to his bride and discovered that his wife, Helen, had eloped with Paris, a prince of Troy.

The Battle of Troy, indeed Troy itself, was long thought of as just part of the fascinating but incredible Greek legends, which scholars have tolerantly called mythology. Troy and the events pertaining to it were still considered to be pure mythological when Charles McLaren suggested, back in 1822, that a certain mound in eastern Turkey, called Hissarlik, was the site of the Homeric Troy. It was only when a businessman named Heinrich Schliemann, risking his own money, came up with spectacular discoveries as he dug up the mound in 1870, that scholars began to acknowledge the existence of Troy. It is now accepted that the Battle of Troy had actually taken place in the thirteenth century BCE. It was then, according to the Greek sources, that Gods and men had fought side by side; in such beliefs the Greeks were not alone.

Acting directly or indirectly, sometimes seen and sometimes unseen, the various gods, nudged the principal actors of this human drama to their fates. Behind it all was Jove (Zeus): "While the other gods and the armed warriors on the plain slept soundly, Jove (Zeus) was wakeful, for he was thinking how to do honor to Achilles and destroy much people at the ships of the Achaeans." Individual gods had their own reasons for whom they favored in the battle. Only Zeus, as the supreme deity and ultimate arbitrator, was impartial. Only he would judge and determine by what rules the combatants fought and who and when others could intervene. When his own son, Saredon, was facing death he would not interfere with the outcome.

Even before the battle was joined, the God Apollo began the hostilities, "He sat himself down away from the ships with a face as dark as night, and his silver bow rang death as he shot his arrow in the midst of them (the Achaeans) … for nine whole days he shot his arrows among the people … and all day long, the pyres of the dead were burning."

Hera, Zeus's wife, took an active personal and maternal interest in the outcome. She took personal affront to the fact that Aphrodite was judged by Trojan Paris to be more beautiful than she. Then a Trojan boy replaced her daughter as a cupbearer to the Gods. After these two affronts she sided with the Greeks and schemed against the Trojans. She even attempted to trick her husband in believing the Trojans had insulted him.

The God of the sea, Poseidon, fully supported the ocean-faring Greeks. Whenever Poseidon has the chance he would assist the Greeks in the fight. Although he was Zeus' brother he did recognize that Zeus was the Supreme Being with both more experienced and authority.

Some of the Gods did favor the Trojans. The twins Apollo and Artemis gave aid to the city of Troy. Apollo was angry with King Agamemnon because he refused to ransom Khryseis, a daughter of one of his priests. He was responsible for sending a plague to the Greeks and he was the first God to make an appearance in the Iliad.

Paris' choice of Aphrodite over Hera, led Hera to support the Trojans and she was successful in convincing Ares, her lover and the God of war, to help the Trojans.

A favorite of the gods was Patroklos, who was killed outside of Troy because he disobeyed Achilles. It had been determined that Patroklos would not be the conqueror of Troy, Apollo did not intervene but protected him. The other Gods simply viewed Apollo's part in the matter as a natural disaster, except for the demigod Achilles, who was angry over the death of Patroklos. So as payback he disgraced Hector's body by tethering the corpse through the ankles and dragging him around Patroklos' tomb every day for twelve days.

The gods were very angry after this barbaric treatment of a hero. Achilles' mother Thetis was sent by Zeus to visit him and implore him to ransom and return the body for proper burial. Achilles acceded to his mother's request and agreed to ransom the body to the Trojans. Even as a demigod, Achilles realized the importance of respecting the wishes of the gods.

The gods had unlimited freedom on the earth and were revered by all humans. The gods themselves were not omniscient and they knew that Zeus eventually would judge their actions, and they would have to answer for them. Zeus acted as a mediator and balanced the actions of Gods and men to ensure that whatever fate decreed happened. When Achilles returned to the battlefield, after leaving because of a disagreement with Agamemnon, the tide of battle swung to the

Greeks. This angered the gods so much that they implored Zeus to allow them to assist the Trojans. They feared that Achilles, being the son of a God, would single handedly win the battle and the war. Therefore, to counter Achilles, Zeus allowed the Gods to once again participate in the battle.

Zeus in his own way did take interest in the events of the battle, but not in a strategic way. He chose instead to deal with the personal lives of individuals. When Patroklos put on Achilles' armor and went out to battle the Trojans he was killed by Hector. Zeus knew that Achilles would revenge Patroklos' death and Hector would die. So, Zeus having compassion for Hector elected to give him an honorable death.

Aphrodite was the Goddess of love, beauty and fertility. She was also a protector of sailors. The poet Hesiod mirrored the above stating that Aphrodite was born from sea-foam. Homer, on the other hand, said that she was the daughter of Zeus and Dione. When Paris, a Trojan prince was asked to choose the most beautiful Olympian Goddess he chose Aphrodite. He did not choose Hera or Athena, who had attempted to bribe him with offers of power and victory in battle. What the two didn't know was that Aphrodite promised Paris the love of the most beautiful woman in the world.

Unfortunately, the most beautiful woman in the world was Helen of Troy, and she was already married to Menelaus, the king. When she eloped with Paris, neither of them realized, that they were the architects of a war that would last for many years, cost thousands of lives, and live on in history forever.

As fate would have it, Hera and Athena were enemies of Troy while Aphrodite was grateful to Paris and the Trojans.

Aphrodite also had a son, Aeneas, who was supporting the Trojans. When he looked as if he would be killed in the battle, Aphrodite intervened and saved her son. The Greek hero Diomedes was Aeneas' opponent and when the goddess intervened he attacked her with his spear. Aphrodite was wounded on the wrist and bled ichor (blood).

Aphrodite was so alarmed by this injury that she dropped Aeneas, who was then rescued by Apollo, the Olympian god. She sought out her brother Ares, the god of war, who lent his chariot to her so that she could fly to Olympus and escape further injury. Her mother Dione then treats her wound, and her father Zeus tells her to leave war to Ares and Athena.

Aphrodite does not heed Zeus' advice and once again enters the battle and saves Paris who was about to be killed by King Menelaus. This time she wraps him in a mist and spirits him away to his own bedroom in Troy. She then informs Helen that Paris is waiting for her. Helen then asks Aphrodite if she being led to ruin once again and even suggests that Aphrodite go to Paris herself. Aphrodite is enraged and yells at Helen, "I'll hate you, as much as I love you now."

Although Aphrodite and Hera, Zeus's wife, support opposite sides in the war, the goddess of love loans Hera her magical girdle in order to distract Zeus. This girdle causes men and Gods to fall hopelessly in love with its wearer. According to Pausanias, an ancient travel writer, a number of statues of Aphrodite dressed in battle dress were in Sparta as well as other Greek centers. She was not a war Goddess, although some have seen her as such and find significance in her pairing with the war God Ares in mythology and worship.

Aeneas was one of the most respected of the Trojan heroes, engaging in single combat with the Greek heroes Diomedes, Idomeneus, and Achilles. Twice he was rescued through the intervention of gods. When the Greeks were sacking Troy, Aeneas fought until he was ordered by the gods to flee. Leaving the city he carried his father and the household gods on his shoulders.

The events that led to the Trojan War started at the royal wedding. Peleus, king of the Myrmidons, was marrying a sea nymph named Thetis. Many gods attended the wedding, but Eris, Zeus' daughter, wasn't invited, because it was feared that the goddess of discord would cause trouble.

True to her label as goddess of discord, on hearing that she was not invited to the wedding she decided to attend it anyway. She brought a golden apple marked with the phrase "for the fairest" and tossed it amongst the guests. The goddesses Hera, Athena and Aphrodite all thought that they were the fairest and deserved the golden apple. They bickered for a while and then asked Zeus to decide the matter.

Zeus realized that he was in a no win situation and decided not to get involved. He sent them to a prince named Paris, the son of King Priam of Troy in Anatolia. He was raised as a simple shepherd because his mother learned in a vision that he would cause the destruction of Troy.

Why did Zeus choose Paris to judge the contest? Was it because Paris had a reputation as being very honest or was it because Zeus realized that he was not smart enough not to get involved with the goddesses. Paris was also known to be a good judge of cattle. Regardless of the reason Paris did get involved, and eventually fell in love with Helen. Now, Helen was a half-mortal daughter of Zeus and many powerful men wanted to marry her. Her stepfather, King Tyndareus of Sparta, was afraid that this competition of suitors would lead to war.

Tyndareus took out an insurance policy against this eventuality by convincing Helen's suitors to swear an oath that they would protect her and her husband, whoever he might be. Then Helen married Menelaus, the brother of Agamemnon, the king of Mycenae. After Tyndareus' death Helen's husband became the king of Sparta.

Paris went to Sparta where Helen lived. He was welcomed as a guest by both Menelaus and Helen. When Menelaus had to leave Sparta for a period, Paris convinced Helen to accompany him to Troy. Returning to Sparta, Menelaus learned that his wife has eloped with his guest Paris. Outraged to hear this news he summoned the princes who had promised to protect Helen, and they agreed to help him get Helen back by going to war against Troy. Menelaus' brother Agamemnon was the leader of the army.

The hero Achilles was also recruited for the war. It was said that he was invincible. According to legend Achilles' mother Thetis dipped him in the River Styx, making him invulnerable to weapons. But to make Achilles' skin invulnerable his mother had to dip him into the river by holding onto his heel. This made Achilles virtually indestructible everywhere except for his heel: thus the expression his "Achilles' heel."

The Greek army was gathered and ready for battle. One thousand Greek ships were loaded with supplies and weapons. There was only one problem: no wind to fill the sails. Agamemnon solved the problem by sacrificing his daughter, Iphigenia, to the Goddess Artemis. The Gods were obviously pleased and the wind returned allowing the Greek ships to set sail for Troy.

To be fair to Helen, her marriage to Menelaus was arranged by her father, and was very political. He had wealth and power and was the brother of the most powerful Greek King Agamemnon. He didn't have the good looks of other suitors but did offer a palace, a kingdom, and security for her entire family.

During the early years of their marriage Sparta was infected with the plague and Menelaus was advised by an oracle to go to Troy to observe propitiatory rites at the graves of Lycus and Chimaereus, sons of Prometheus. Menelaus obeyed and went to Troy where he met Paris, who had accidentally killed his best friend in an athletic contest and needed purification.

The two returned to Sparta and Paris had the opportunity to see the beautiful Helen on many occasions. He knew that it was she that had been promised to him by Aphrodite. Menelaus suddenly had to leave Sparta for Crete to attend his grandfather's funeral ceremonies. Innocently, he left the handsome visitor to be entertained by his wife. Helen was completely charmed by the stranger. Paris was handsome, but Aphrodite, to guarantee success of her project made him even more beautiful. He possessed manners and charm. It was impossible for Helen not to fall in love with this young man. And Paris had fallen in love with Helen instantly, proving the adage 'Love at first sight.'

Apparently, Menelaus had not been gone long before the two lovers left for Troy. Paris had his own ship and his own retainers and crew. Helen also had her own attendants; some say Paris robbed the royal treasury with Helen's help. It does not speak too well for Menelaus' authority that his security forces would have allowed this flagrant plundering.

Those loyal to Menelaus claimed that Helen was taken by force. Another version blamed the Goddess Aphrodite: claiming that she deceived Helen by changing the appearance of Paris to look like Menelaus.

On the return voyage to Troy, Paris erected a sanctuary at Gythium to the Goddess Aphrodite, who might otherwise give them trouble at a later time.

At this time Paris had not slept with Helen. She had kept him at bay while they were in Greece, but once on the open sea biological urges caused Paris to drop anchor and consummate their new, but predestined relationship.

The mating must have been remarkable for both of them. Paris now had his dreams fulfilled—he was making love to the most beautiful woman in the world, and Helen who had only had sex with two men: the aging Theseus and the prosaic Menelaus. Now she was experiencing a virile young man who must have given her the bliss she had only imagined.

At last they arrived in Troy. The inhabitants of the city, even those who had criticized the recklessness of Paris, could only marvel at the divine beauty that stepped off the ship with him. Almost immediately a wedding ceremony took place, and it was as though Helen had never been married. Even Paris' father, Priam was fully won over and vowed to protect her as long as she remained in Troy.

Couriers brought news of the betrayal of both Helen and Paris to Menelaus in Crete. Agamemnon was furious. Not only was his family dishonored, but also he felt personally insulted.

Agamemnon consulted the oracle at Delphi before getting involved in a war against Troy.

Menelaus, Odysseus, and Acamas, the son of Theseus went to Troy. Though counseled by such advisers as Antenor and Aeneas to surrender Helen, Priam stubbornly refused. He remembered when Heracles and Telamon kidnapped his sister Hesione. He had beseeched the Greeks to return his sister, and his entreaties were ignored and his pleas fell on deaf ears.

The envoys returned to Greece, and preparations for war began.

When all is said and done, Helen of Troy is just a story about two great cities being betrayed by their rulers and by their gods. Helen, for her part, was an adulteress who not only abandoned her husband, but also her four children. She was merely a pawn in a master chess game played by Zeus and the other gods. At best, Paris was a simple-minded egotist, who cared nothing for his parents or his citizenry. His only thought was for himself and the woman he needed to fulfill his life. Neither character really understood or cared about the people who were dying daily as a result of their indiscretions. In fact, Helen seemed almost oblivious to the horrors that surrounded her. She displayed very little emotion and showed no visible remorse. Helen was unaffected by the outcome of the war, and didn't acknowledge the sacrifice paid by virtually every family in Greece.

Ever since the first war of gods and men, when Ra and Horus battled Seth for Egypt, it was believed that the wars of men were not only decreed by the gods, but they were also fought with the Gods' active participation.

In the epic Greek tale Kypria, we discover that the Trojan War was caused directly by the god Zeus. The Kypria informs us that, "there was a time when thousands upon thousands of men encumbered the broad bosom of the earth. And having pity on them, Zeus in his great wisdom resolved to lighten Earth's burden. So he caused the strife at Ilion (Troy) to that end; that through death he might make a void in the race of men."

The famous Greek storyteller, Homer, records the Helen of Troy tale in his book the Iliad and states that the war can be blamed on gods, who manipulated the principle antagonists, through direct and indirect means.

In fact, it was Zeus who was the major architect of the war: while other gods and the armed warriors on the plain slept soundly, Jove (Zeus) was wakeful for he was thinking how to do honor to Achilles and destroy much people at the ships of the Achaeans.

Many of the combatants were Greek and Trojan heroes, and the gods and goddesses watched their individual mortal struggles carefully as they were their sons as a result of mating with humans. The fighting was so unpredictable and the risk of injury and death so imminent that the gods and goddesses entered the foray protecting their offspring and punishing opposing gods and their warriors. The fighting grew so intense that Zeus called for a truce and ordered the gods to stay out the fight to avoid personal injury to themselves and other gods.

However, the truce was short-lived, because the gods could not stand by and see injury or death befall their children. The god Mars, after witnessing the death of his son Ascalaphus, at the hands of a Achaean cried, "Do not blame me, ye Gods that dwell in heaven, if I go to the ships of the Achaeans and avenge the death of my son, even if in the end I shall be struck by Jove's (Zeus) lightning and shall lie in blood and dust among the corpses."

Achilles and Agamemnon argued, and Achilles refused to fight any longer; Patroclus donned his armor and took his place and was killed by Hector (who also took Achilles' armor). Enraged, Achilles killed Hector (after his mother acquired new armor from Hephaestus and Hector was injured by Ajax) and dragged his body around Troy three times before allowing Priam (Hector's father and King of Troy) to bury it.

Achilles was a demigod, who initially refused to fight in the battle, now changed his mind and joined the Achaeans. According to Homer, as long as the gods didn't interfere in the battle the Achaeans with Achilles were victorious. Shortly after the death of Hector, Achilles defeated Memnon of Ethiopia, Cygnus of Colonae, and the Amazon warrior Penthesilia (with whom Achilles also had an affair in some versions). He was very soon after killed by Paris—either by an arrow to the heel, or in an older version by a knife to the back (or heel) while visiting a Trojan princess, Polyxena during a truce. Both versions conspicuously deny the killer any sort of valor, and Achilles remains undefeated on the battle-field. His bones are mingled with those of Patroclus, and funeral games are held. Like Ajax, he is represented as living after his death in the island of Leuke at the mouth of the Danube.

Zeus seeing that the tide of the battle had changed as a result of the participation of demigods, decided to wash his hands of the whole affair and said to the gods and goddesses, "For my own part, I shall stay here, seated on Mount Olympus, and look on in peace. But you others, do go among the Trojans and Achaeans, and help either side as you might be disposed."

So finally Zeus showed his true colors for all to see. He didn't care which side won, he only wanted the battles, indeed the war to continue. Blood was blood: god, demigod or human. Call it by its name or call it ambrosia. This 'life-force' was spilled, soaking, saturating the earth which covered the battlefield, which was littered with stacks of broken and splintered shields, spears, lances, arrows and bows and piles of bent, rusting, swords, knives and helmets.

Zeus was known in the Bible as God, the Yahweh, also known by the Sumerians and the Babylonians as Anu. The Norse people called him Odin. The Romans referred to Zeus as Jupiter. And the Hittites called their version of Zeus, Teshub, which meant "Storm God Whose Strength Makes Dead."

The Greeks were growing very tiresome of this struggle. After having laid siege to Troy for approximately ten years, they were still unable to breach the impenetrable city walls. So as a last resort, the Greeks decided to trick the Trojans, since traditional warfare had been unsuccessful. Their plan was to build a tribute to Troy, a massive offering to convince the Trojans that they had left were paying respect.

They chose to build a huge wooden horse that was hollowed out, and asked the artist Epeius to build it. A group of Greek heroes, including Odysseus climbed inside the horse and waited. Meanwhile, the army boarded their ships and sailed toward Greece. One man Sinon was left behind. He claimed to be disillusioned by the purpose of the war and had deserted. Although he was questioned by the Trojans, who despite being warned by those not so gullible, believed his tale and welcomed the tribute. The Trojans celebrated what they thought was their victory, and dragged the wooden horse into Troy.

That night, after a night of celebration, most of Troy was asleep. Sinon, then let the Greek warriors out of the horse, and using surprise as their biggest weapon, attacked the Trojans slaughtering them. The Trojan men were killed and their women raped.

14

The God King Called 'The Stormer'

"You may triumph on the fields of Pelennor for a day,
  But against the Power that has now arisen there is no victory,"
said Gandalf to Aragorn in his tent outside of the city of Gondor.

The god Kings of Sumer moved to other nearby regions of the Middle-east and one Teshub, who was said to be of 'Heaven and Earth,' became the god King of the Hittites in what is now Turkey.

These gods had the authority to appoint human kings and taught them in the ways of war, treaties, and diplomatic affairs. Teshub, and other olden gods were pictured as wearing goggles and appeared on rocket-like objects. The 'goggles' became the Hittite symbol for 'divine' or 'heavenly god.' 2 There is also an epic tale that also tells of their rulers being 'king in heaven' and of coming to 'dark-hued Earth.'

There is an interesting tale surrounding Teshub that claims that he had to defeat a monster named Yanka. Now Yanka, translates as 'serpent,' and was also a god. So, Teshub had competition for the job as god King before he could establish himself as absolute ruler. The story goes that Teshub had to battle Yanka in hand to hand combat. Neither side could prevail, so Teshub requested that other gods come to his aid. Only one goddess helped and after getting Yanka drunk they were able to kill him. This tale of the combat was titled, "The Myth of the Slaying of the Dragon." This ancient story may well be the origin for the medieval tale of "St. George and the Dragon."

When the gods couldn't settle disputes among themselves and chose not to settle the matter through mortal combat they would ask the 'Assembly of the gods' to adjudicate the matter. These original olden gods, the Anunnaki of Sumer: Anu, Enki and Enlil, and the rest would advise and in some cases instruct the petitioner on how to use the old weapons, such as the Olden Copper Lance (missile) to defeat an enemy. Ancient tales tell of Teshub requesting advanced weapons from the Assembly.

Armed with such knowledge and weapons the Hittite army was virtually invincible and was led by a king with the name 'Stormer.'

Those opposing the coming onslaught of The God King Called 'The Stormer' and the Hittite army undoubtedly echoed Gandalf's warnings of doom and despair. Such was the reputation of the Hittite army, that the very thought of their assault caused nations to sue for peace.

The Hittites Empire was vast, stretching from Mesopotamia to Syria and Palestine. It had expanded for hundreds of years and based its expansion on orders from its supreme God TESHUB. The Hittites referred to their supreme God as the 'Storm God Whose Strength Makes Dead.' This catchy phrase was actually coined by witnesses who claimed that the supreme God took an active role in the battles and was aided by his goddess ISHTAR, who was known as the "Lady of the battlefield."

The Hittites were a Spartan-like people and their warriors were infamous for their ferocity. They are credited with the creation of iron, which they used to forge weapons. Their battle tactics including siege weapons were so advanced that many nations adopted them.

If it had not been for archeology the Hittite civilization would still be almost unknown. Excavations in the 19th century provided evidence of the importance of the Hittite culture. As it has been since time began history is written by the conquerors. The Hittites left very few clues about themselves, their history or their accomplishments. As a direct result of archaeologists and historians, the true greatness of the Hittites did not begin to surface until the 20th century.

The original home of the Hittites was Hatti and the land was called Hatti-land.

One of the greatest Hittite kings was Suppilulimas who reigned between 1380BCE and 1340 BCE. It was he who led the Hittite armies and assimilated much from the Sumerian civilization.

The Egyptians regarded the Hittites as barbarians. Both countries waged war for one hundred years, which drained the resources of both.

Expanding a country's borders, feeding and clothing a large army was a great expense that could only be justified by gaining money and resources from the conquered foe.

One of the largest economic resources in the Near East was in the Syria region. This explains why so many neighboring kingdoms coveted this land.

Syria was the hub of the ancient world of commerce. If you needed a product or building materials you had to come to Syria. The expression that all roads lead to Rome was predated by a thousand years because all trade routes led to Syria. If you needed raw materials such as precious metals, tin, copper, lapis lazuli, and other merchandise from as far away as Iran and Afghanistan you could find it in Syria.

The Hittites created a very unique empire, in that after conquering a nation, they simply added that nation's gods to their own. This was a very diplomatic move resulting in reducing the emotional stress suffered by the conquered people.

Therefore it is not surprising that the Hittites adopted many of the Sumerian and Babylonian gods. This inclusion of foreign gods had tremendous consequences for the history of the Hebrews. The Hittites Empire in Mesopotamia survived 400 years, from 1600BCE to 1200 BCE. Their civilization ended almost overnight when the Assyrians invaded and their army completely overran them. The Assyrians went on to Palestine and destroyed the Jewish State. The Assyrians adopted the Hittites tradition of including the gods of conquered peoples into their hierarchy of gods allowing the Jewish survivors the right to worship their Hebrew god, Yahweh. This led to a major religious schism between Jews and Samaritans. As a result and after thousands of years there are still Samaritans alive today.

King Suppilulimas' earliest campaign was the invasion of Syria. His tactics totally surprised the Syrians and city after city fell in quick succession. His army was like a plague of locusts that swarmed over the country and climaxed in the sacking of the capital city of Washukkanni.

This assault resulted in the destruction of the balance of power in the region. This was followed almost immediately by a move that surprised all nations that were hoping to gain territory and power from the expected resulting vacuum. Suppilulimas signed a peace treaty with its greatest threats, Egypt and the Kingdom of Mitanni.

The Hittite army, like all late Bronze Age armies, was comprised mostly of infantry and chariots. The majority of the fighting men were seasonal soldiers, in that when not assisting the king in martial campaigns, they were working their lands, planting, and harvesting crops.

What made the Hittite forces unique and helped fuel their reputation as being ferocious warriors, was the fact that they employed mercenaries. These highly trained troops, for the most part, did not receive remuneration from the king. They chose instead to be paid in booty: allowing them license to steal anything of value from their defeated foes.

The Hittite chariot was one of their greatest military achievements. It was much larger and stronger than contemporary chariots, and could be utilized very much like cavalry troops in the eighteenth and nineteenth centuries. As an assault weapon this chariot was used to break lines of attacking infantry, opening huge gaps that could be quickly filled by Hittite warriors that slaughtered retreating troops who were mad with panic and fear.

Because of their battle tactics employing heavy chariots, the Hittites needed wide-open areas to employ their strategies. Therefore, they were very reluctant to attack an enemy in anything but ideal situations.

Suppilulimas, as king of the Hittites, must have been of royal blood. His queen carried the mitochondria DNA of the matrilineal succession, which proved his office as well as his royal lineage as well of that of his siblings.

The god King Called 'The Stormer' caused fear to rise up in the hearts of his enemies, but no one could have predicted the utter panic that ensued with the destruction of the earth by fire and water.

15

The Truth Behind the Destruction of the Earth

The Bible tells us that when man began to increase in number on the earth and when they had daughters that the sons of God saw that the daughters of men were beautiful and as a result married them and had children by them. So God decided, not to punish his sons, but to punish man by limiting his life span to 120 years.

The Nephilim, the sons of God (angels), stems from the Semitic root NFL ('to be cast down'), it means exactly what it says: It means those who were cast down upon Earth.

The Bible goes on to tell us that the Lord believed that Man was wicked and that the thoughts of his heart were only filled with evil. This apparently pained God and he grieved as a result of his creation.

"I will wipe mankind, whom I have created, from the face of the earth—men and animals, and creatures that move along the ground, and birds of the air—for I am grieved that I have made them," said the Lord.

Luckily, as Genesis relates, Noah found favor in the eyes of the Lord. The Lord said to Noah, "Go into the ark, you and your whole family because I have found you righteous in this generation. Take with you seven of every kind of clean animal, a male and its mate, and two of every kind of unclean animal, a male and its mate, and also seven of every kind of bird, male and female, to keep their various kinds alive throughout the earth. Seven days from now I will send rain on the earth for forty days and forty nights, and I will wipe from the face of the earth every living creative I have made."

So Noah obeyed the Lord and he and his family entered the ark, which the Lord had instructed Noah to build. He gathered the creatures of the earth and he waited the seven days for the rain to begin. The rains came and covered the earth for forty days and forty nights.

This tale of the Great Flood, the story of Noah and the ark, specifically the reason the Lord gives for destroying most of life on earth just doesn't make any sense. If it were as simple as he states, then why didn't he punish his sons as well as Man? Do you destroy entire races of creatures just because Man had sex with the sons of God? Or is there more to this story. If we go back earlier in Genesis we realize that Adam and Eve only learned about sex after eating of the forbidden fruit. "Then the eyes of both of them were opened, and they realized they were naked; so they sewed fig leaves together and made coverings for themselves."

So it seems that Mankind was introduced to sex, and that the sons of the Lord came to earth and made love to the daughters of men. Children were born and they mated and the cycle of life continued between the sons of the Lord (Gods) and the heroes of man (demigods) and of the humans.

It doesn't make sense that the Lord destroyed Man because they enjoyed having sex. Was there a more basic and more reasonable motive for the destruction? Once again in Genesis, the Lord spoke, 'My spirit shall not shield Man forever; having strayed, he is but flesh.' What does the Lord mean by 'flesh' and was he concerned with man's morals or of the defilement of the gods?

Now, if we take this into context with this book and realize that mankind was created by genetically altering the genetic code of his/her DNA, we are left with the very real possibility that the Lord was angry because the bloodlines of the gods and those of Man were being corrupted. And because of Man's propensity for having sex with every female he saw, God could be forgiven for believing that Man was no better than that of the animals.

When the Lord called Noah a righteous man he could have meant, "pure in his genealogies." "By intermarrying with the men and women of decreasing genetic purity, the gods were subjecting themselves, too, to deterioration," states Zecharia Sitchin, author of *The 12th Planet*.

Before Genesis there were the Sumerian texts from which the Biblical version of the Great Deluge has been adopted, but as always the many gods have been replaced by the one God. Archaeological discoveries of the Mesopotamian civilization have made it possible to read Akkadian and Sumerian literature. One Akkadian text tells the amazing story of Gilgamesh who relates the original flood story.

Gilgamesh meets King Ziusudra who tells him of the secret of the Great Flood. He told him about a meeting in which the councils of the gods voted on the destruction of Mankind. Their vote and decision was supposed to be kept secret. Enki searched out Utnapishtim/Noah, the ruler of Shuruppak, to inform him of the approaching calamity. Adopting clandestine methods, Enki spoke to Utnapishtim from behind a reed screen.

Enki told Utnapishtim/Noah, to teardown his house and to build a boat. He warned him to forgo his possessions and to care only for his life. Enki then instructed him to gather the seed (DNA) of all living things and to put them aboard the boat. He then dictated the dimensions of the craft that was to be built.

In contrast to the above history that Enki warned Utnapishtim/Noah of the approaching flood, we find other evidence that claims Ea (his father) as the god who—in defiance of the decision of the 'Assembly of the gods'—enabled a trusted follower (the Mesopotamian "Noah") to escape the disaster. Ea is portrayed as the deity that is Mankind's greatest benefactor, the god who brought about civilization.

The Anunnaki appointed the kings of Sumer before the Flood. Following the Flood, kingship was bestowed from heaven to the first human kings. The 'Assembly of the gods' under the presidency of Anu appointed these kings and their role was to act as a shepherd to protect and direct the people.

In the Epic of Gilgamesh we find that the Flood was decreed by the Anunnaki, including Ea, Enki and Enlil and was an attempt, albeit drastic, at population control. The Mesopotamian account of the Flood claims that there was a rampant population problem and that humans were so noisy that Enlil could not sleep.

Enki's follower Utnapishtim told the people of the Mesopotamia that he could no longer live there, and that he had to build a boat to sail to southern Africa to dwell with his God Ea. He even got his neighbors to help in the construction by claiming that the land, which had just undergone a drought, would be rejuvenated and produce large crops. He also fed them red and white wine, bullocks and sheep daily. Even children were enlisted in the cause and as a result of the community assisting in the project—the ark was completed in seven days.

We mentioned that the vote of the council was kept secret: we now know the details of the assembly. Of the five Sumerian poems relating to Gilgamesh that have been discovered, one is entitled 'The Deluge' as experienced by King Ziusudra. In it, details relating to the meeting of the 'Assembly of the gods' are given. The vote was taken and there was a majority of the council decided to destroy mankind but the vote was not unanimous. Nin-khursag, the Lady of Life, voted against destroying mankind. As we already know Enki warned Ziusudra and the ark was built. What is really interesting about this telling of the flood story is the Ziusudra is the 'preserver of the seed of mankind.'

The matter of this preservation is more fully covered in the Babylonian account, which explains that the boat or ark was actually a submarine and it carried seeds of living creatures. In other words, this underwater vehicle carried the DNA of all living things, and was not so much a floating zoo as a floating laboratory.

Clay tablets have been found that list names of kings from after the Deluge. A king was exalted as "of seed preserved from before the Deluge." Therefore although most of mankind was destroyed the bloodline continued....

Dogon mythology states that the Jackal, a failed example of genetic manipulation of primitive man, stole a spaceship from the Nummo, an amphibious race from the Sirius star system, and accidentally crashed the craft into the earth setting off a gigantic nuclear explosion.

Evidence in world mythology indicates that the Nummo did know in advance about the world flood that followed the cataclysm. Several individuals were warned ahead of time about the flood. This indicates that the flood may have been created by the Nummo to clean away the toxins and to put out the fires caused by the holocaust. Many old and modern civilizations realize the importance of rain and flooding as purifiers of the land.

Ancient Egyptians talk about flooding and fire as two of the most common causes of destruction. This is particularly interesting because it relates directly to the Dogon oral history concerning the Nummo and the destruction of the earth.

They also mention the fact that after a flood those living close to the water in the cities are killed, and only shepherds and herdsmen who live in the mountains survive. Unfortunately, they are destitute of letters and education so the civilization has to begin all over again. This is important as it relates to the Dogon tribe who live high in the Cliffs of Bandiagara. They claim their oral history comes from the beginning of time.

After the destruction of the earth the Nummo return to earth from the granary to regenerate man and clean the land. The granary housed the DNA that was used to create man and edible plants.

The similarities between the Sumerian mythology and the Dogon mythology are numerous. In this mythology Ea appeared in remote times, when humans lived like beast just as the Nummo did in Dogon mythology. He was part fish and part man, and was said to have had two heads, identifying his androgynous nature. He instructed humans in handicrafts, farming, letters, laws, architecture, and magic. He softened the primitive rudeness of humans and since that time nothing has been added to improve on his teaching. He also retired to the sea and was seen to be amphibious, being able to survive in water and on land like the Nummo.

The Sumerian god Enki is associated with the Nummo. He was the one that instructed Ziusudra to build the ark and escape the flood. Enki was the son of Ea who was known as the "lord of the house of water." He ruled the ocean of sweet water on which the world floated. His priests wore garments in the form of fish.

In Greek mythology when Prometheus was chained to the rock, Zeus sent a great flood. Zeus was disgusted to see how wicked man had become and decided to destroy them. Prometheus warned his son, Deucalion, about Zeus' intentions and told him to build an ark. So he, his wife Pyrrha, the daughter of Epimehteus and Pandora, and their children boarded the boat.

Zeus, with Poseidon's help, sent rain from the heavens and flooded the world. It rained for nine days and nine nights before Ducalion's boat landed on Mount Parnassus. They looked out to see that there was no sign of life anywhere. Zeus took pity on them and drained the floodwaters. They ventured down and found a slimy temple where they entered to give thanks.

Zeus then sent Hermes and Themis to tell them to veil their heads and cast the bones of their mother over their shoulders. In this case, mother meant 'Mother Earth,' and the bones were stones. The ones Deucalion threw became men and the stones Pyrrha threw became women.

In the 1920's Leonard Woolley and his team of archaeologists discovered the first pre-Flood remains of old Mesopotamia. At the time of the flood Mesopotamia was considered the center of the world, so if a flood were to cover all of Mesopotamia and the surrounding areas, it would have been considered a worldwide flood.

Anyway, after six years of excavations Woolley found an intriguing complex of ancient graves plus a stone-built tomb that dated back 3500 BCE. What was interesting was that there is no stone in this desert area. In fact not even a pebble can be found within 48 kilometers of the site. When they entered the stone-built tomb they discovered golden goblets, fine ornaments decorated with chips of red limestone and lapis lazuli, bronze tableware, silver jewelry, and much more. Surrounding this treasure soldiers were buried with helmets, spears and shields. Also, buried were attendants; the remains of ladies in crimson robes, with ornate head-dresses, golden earrings and silver combs.

These attendants and soldiers were guarding the tombs of Queen Shrub-ad and her husband A-bar-gi.

More tombs, more treasure was found but the quest for proof of the flood had eluded them.

The archaeologists continued excavating digging carefully into the ground and the past. They arrived at the time of Abraham, and then after another 1000 years the time of Noah but still no flood evidence. They sunk shafts deeper through dozens of feet of rubble when suddenly they came upon wood-ash and several inscribed clay tablets. Woolley had himself lowered to this depth but instead of standing on bedrock he was standing on solid clay. This was the type of clay that can only be deposited by water. So they continued to dig down a further eight feet through the clay and then it abruptly ended. This soil was perfect for all types of irrigation. It was the foundation of the 'Fertile Crescent.' Pottery, jars, bowls, and other evidence of human habitation was found. Below this soil was more clay and when it was analyzed it contained fossils of marine life from before the flood. It now could be established that the great flood of Noah had occurred over six thousand years ago.

Woolley sent a telegram to London with the news: *We have found the Flood.*

16

Viracocha—After the Deluge

There are legends, told by the peoples of the Andes that tall, bearded, pale-skinned men came to Peru shortly after a terrible deluge had covered the earth, and nearly destroyed mankind. These men were led by a leader the natives called Viracocha, and it was said that he came in a time of chaos to set the world right.

One legend describes Viracocha as being accompanied by 'messengers' of two kinds: 'faithful soldiers' (huaminca) and 'shining ones' (hayhawy). Their role was said to be to carry the message of Viracocha to all parts of the world.

It is believed that these white-men constructed ancient cities such as Cuzco, and built the nearby citadel of Sacsayhuaman. This citadel was built using large stones, which had been cut out of rock and positioned (balanced) delicately on rows of equally enormous stone. Some of these stones weigh more than 300 tons, while others average more than 100 tons each.

Available evidence points to the fact that the Inca stonemasons had sufficient skills to repair and maintain these ancient structures, but did not have the knowledge to create new buildings or cities.

Peru has a network of roads that stretch for over 15,000 miles. These roads of surfaced track parallel each other. One road runs adjacent to the coastline, while another mirrors it by zigzagging its way through the Andes Mountains. Once again, the locals claim that tradition cites the builders of these roads as being the Viracochas: bearded, white-haired strangers.

Viracocha was credited with changing all this with initiating the long-lost golden age, which later generations looked back on with nostalgia. All the legends agreed, furthermore, that he had carried out his civilizing mission with great kindness and as far as possible had abjured the use of force: careful instruction and personal example had been the main methods used to equip the people with the techniques and knowledge necessary for a cultured and productive life. In particular, he was remembered for bringing to Peru such varied skills as medicine, metallurgy, farming, animal husbandry, the art of writing, and a sophisticated understanding of the principals of engineering and architecture.

The mystery was deepened by local traditions which stated not only that the road system and the sophisticated architecture had been "ancient in the time of the time of the Incas," but that both "were the work of the white, auburn-haired men" who had lived thousands of years earlier.

In the life of Manco Capac, who was the first Inca, and from whom they began to boast themselves children of the Sun, and from whom they derived their idolatrous worship of the Sun, they had an ample account of the deluge. They say that in it perished all races of men and created things insomuch that the waters rose above the highest mountain peaks in the world. No living thing survived except a man and a woman who remained in a box (ark) and, when the waters subsided, the wind carried them … to Tiahuanaco [where] the creator began to raise up the people and the nations that are in that region … Is this, as Zecharia Sitchin suggests, proof that the deluge or Noah's Flood, occurred prior to the creation of Adam and Eve, as he postulates in his book *The 12th Planet*. Are the occupants of the box, Adam and Eve, or Noah, his wife, and children plus thousands of animals?

The Peruvian Indians believe that they were created after a great flood had engulfed their entire land. All the men living at that time drown. Their creator had caused the flood and then appeared in human form and was called Viracocha. It was claimed that he arrived on the shores of Lake Titicaca and made the city of Tiahuanaco temporarily his home. He then created the heavens including the sun, moon and stars. After moving to the city of Cuzco, Viracocha created Man The story cited about the creation of the earth and of the Peruvian Indians is very reminiscent to the creation myth in the book of Genesis.

These giants were the Angels of the Book of Enoch and the Nephilim from the Bible, but also the Anunnaki from ancient Sumer. Remember, that when they descended from Heaven to Earth, they mated with the women of mankind and the women bore them children. We have already read that the giants had intercourse with animals and that these admonitions created unspeakable horrors that crept upon the earth. This was one of the reasons given by the Gods for causing the great deluge to cover the earth and destroy mankind. Is it possible that the Anunnaki built another spaceport in Peru to explore South America for the purpose of mining gold? Many archaeologists believe that Machu Picchu was built in the 15th century. According to Rolf Muller, a professor of Astronomy at the University of Potsdam claims to have found evidence that proves that Machu Picchu is much older and in fact was built between 4000 and 2000 BCE. Professor

Muller states that he based his conclusions on astronomical alignments that were observable from Machu Picchu in its distant past.

17

The Untold Story of Gilgamesh

Artist's depiction of Izapa Tree.

Archaeologists in Iraq believe they may have found the lost tomb of King Gilgamesh, the hero of the oldest 'book' in history. If true, this is an incredible discovery, for Gilgamesh was far more than a man, he was the son of a god. This discovery could tell us much about the hierarchy of the Sumerian Gods, for Gilgamesh was not only a king but also a judge of the Anunnaki.

The tale the Epic of Gilgamesh was discovered, written on twelve clay tablets in cuneiform script. The discovered tablets are now known as the Shin-eqi-unninni tablets and were excavated in 1839 by Austen Henry Layard. In total Layard discovered some twenty-five thousand clay tablets. They were found in the ruins of Nineveh, which was the capital of the Assyrian Empire. Today, the ancient site of Nineveh is part of Mosul, the second largest city in modern Iraq.

The Epic of Gilgamesh is about the adventures of the historical King of Uruk who lived approximately between 2750 and 2500 BCE. Unlike Greek mythology, the hero of The Epic of Gilgamesh was an actual historical figure. When Gilgamesh died his people continued to worship him. In life, he was a living god and in death he joined the Parthenon of Sumerian deities. One prayer, of particular interest, invokes him as, "Gilgamesh, supreme king, judge of the Anunnaki". Gilgamesh believed he was two-thirds god and one-third human. His mother was the goddess Ninsun and his father was the high priest of Kullab.

The Gilgamesh stories are just part of a much larger literary discovery. Versions of which survive not only in Akkadian, a Semitic language related to Hebrew and spoken by the Babylonians, but also on tablets written in Hurrian and Hittite. All these languages were written in the script known as cuneiform, which means, 'wedge-shaped.'

In The Epic of Gilgamesh we are informed that Gilgamesh did not want to die—ever. Being part god he believed he had the birth right to immorality. He also had knowledge that if he entered into a Holy Land, a forbidden place in the Cedar Mountains of Lebanon, he had an opportunity to gain immortality.

The Tall Cedars of Lebanon seem to have secret or forgotten knowledge associated with them: apparently descendants of the Nephilim believe that the cedars are symbolically significant to their language, and there is a Masonic side degree called the "Tall Cedars of Lebanon."

One of his many journeys was with Enkidu who was sent by Ninsun (mother and goddess of Gilgamesh) to try and convince Gilgamesh that he was, indeed, mortal and there was nothing that he could do about this inevitable fate.

Enkidu was a wild animal-like man full of hair and described as looking like a two-legged lion with hair all over his body. This half-ape creature of a man had lived most of his life alone or with wild animals in the woods. Nobles of Uruk tamed him by assigning him to a harlot for making relentless love to women in an almost continuous cycle.

Ninsun had him reassigned to a camp near the town where he was taught in the manners of speech, civilization and told of the habits of Gilgamesh. When he was ready, he confronted Gilgamesh in the hope of bringing him to his senses.

Their confrontation occurred in Uruk when Gilgamesh was roaming the streets looking for sexual adventures. Enkidu confronted him and would not let him pass. This resulted in a physical battle between these two mighty men and eventually ended up as a stalemate with both respecting the other and they became very good friends.

Gilgamesh explained to Enkidu that he wanted to go to the land of Tilmun in search of his quest—Enkidu agreed to accompany and safeguard him. They then set out together in search of this very secret and secure location that was forbidden to all mortals and known as Shamash in the Cedar Mountain region. His objective was to obtain a Shem, which was the vehicle (that flew) used for obtaining immortality.

He also knew about the Huwawa, which guarded this land of the missiles. Gilgamesh brought special weapons and strategies in preparation of this obstruction. This 'mechanical monster' that they were about to confront was a technological marvel and a deadly opponent.

After traveling for a long time they arrived at the "Place where the Rising is Made." They are both physically and mentally exhausted and fall asleep. Enkidu wakes Gilgamesh because an overpowering light and the sounds of a landslide disturbed him. Gilgamesh glanced around and seeing or hearing nothing fell back to sleep. What Enkidu may have described was the launching of a spacecraft. It was this awareness that caused Gilgamesh to believe that they were near his objection—the 'landing place.' The next morning they found the gate to Tilmun. Enkidu attempted to open it but received such an electrical shock that he was paralyzed for twelve days. Once recovered, he begged Gilgamesh to reconsider, and not enter the forbidden land.

However, Gilgamesh had found a new passage that incorporated a tunnel that had no gate or other defenses. He thought that once the entrance and tunnel were cleared of debris they could easily enter the land unseen and unharmed.

They had just started clearing the debris when they were confronted by a very angry creature with 'mighty teeth like a dragon' and his face "like a lion with a beam emanating from his forehead." His name was Huwawa and his task was to guard this land. The God Shamash, with Ishtar (Inanna) watching, intervenes in the outcome and saves Gilgamesh when it appears he will be slain. Huwawa was armed with seven cloaks, but was only wearing one. Shamash advises Gilgamesh and Enkidu to see this as an advantage, and instead of fleeing from the monster, they attack. Huwawa fires a beam that destroys the land around them, but they are left unharmed.

Shamash creates a devastating wind to encircle Huwawa, which causes his beam weapon to malfunction. Enkidu and Gilgamesh confront Huwawa. A ferocious struggle ensues. With axe and sword they strike Huwawa and eventually he falls and is killed by Gilgamesh. Although Huwawa is destroyed—Gilgamesh does not gain immortality.

Another tale of Gilgamesh was translated from the clay tablets. Without the successful translation of this story the twelfth tablet could not have been deciphered. This story was the key. It's called "Gilgamesh and the Huluppu Tree," and it holds the first literary reference to Lilith.

Lilith was Adam's first wife and he insisted that she always lie below him during sex. She believed that she was equal to Adam and complained to him. When her complaints weren't addressed she sought help from God and was once again ignored, so she flew away. As punishment she was transformed into a demon of the air and is alleged to be responsible for killing infants in their cradles. When she fled the Garden, God sent three angels to bring her back. She didn't want to return to the status quo and disobeyed God. So he had his angels kill 100 of her children daily until she returned.

She was also accused of seducing men in their sleep and forcing them into sex. Apparently, she needed the semen to give birth to more demons.

The reference to Lilith contained in the tale "Gilgamesh and the Huluppu Tree," is the key to understanding the twelfth tablet where the first twelve lines are almost completely broken away. Without the explanation offered in the "Huluppu Tree," the 12th tablet could not be read.

Still another story tells us about Gilgamesh and the Great Flood. According to the story, a man named Utnapishtim said to Gilgamesh that he would tell him a secret known only to deities. He asked him if he knew of the city of Shuruppak, on the banks of the Euphrates. It was here, according to Utnapishtim, that the Gods decided to destroy mankind. Ea, a God of the Sumerians had come to his house and warned him about the impending flood and had him build a ship and to bring aboard the ship the seed of all living beings.

Utnapishtim is actually Noah of the Book of Genesis. He answers Ea that he understands and acknowledges that it is a great honor. However, he wonders what he is to say to people in the city and to the city council when they ask why he is building a boat? Ea said to tell them that Enlil hates him and that he has to leave and travel to where Apsu and Ea Live. Utnapishtim also mentioned that Enlil will send rain to water their crops after he leaves. He adds that edible birds will fall from the sky, delicious fish will jump from the canals onto the land, and in the evening showers of grain would fall.

The people of the city were so impressed by Utnapishtim's prophecies that they came and helped build the ship. Carpenters, reed-workers, and children carried the pitch and strong men fetched the heavy things.

Supplies had been gathered from far and wide and now it was time to begin to build the frame of the craft. The dimensions were 60 meters long, 60 meters wide and 60 meters high. It was a perfect cube. It was not a boat, as we know them today. The hull was not long and narrow but square. The floor space occupied an entire acre.

It had an upper deck and six lower decks. It was more a passenger liner than a lifeboat. The only question that remains unanswered was who were the passengers?

18

Legacy of the Elf-Queens

Illustration of Elf-Queen.

The Elves and Men of Middle-earth were friends. More importantly they were allies and considered themselves equal. Man learned much from the wisdom of the Elves. They grew so close that Elves and Men became lovers and had children. Elrond, the father of Arwen, was born as a result of the mating of an Elf and a mortal.

Tolkien wrote and we saw it in the trilogy of movies, that Elrond, king of Rivendell, desperately attempted to end the relationship his daughter the Lady Arwen, was having with Lord Aragorn, the heir to the throne of Gondor, the king of the West. What is ironic about this interference is the fact that the birth of Elrond himself was as a result of an elf and mortal mating. This information unfortunately is only told in *The Silmarillion*.

In the Celtic world, certain royal families were said to carry the fairy blood, that is to say, the fate or destiny of the royal bloodline, while the elf princesses of romance and history were often called 'self-maidens'. Certain royal families were said to carry the fairy blood, and it was their responsibility to safeguard the royal blood, but not only for their family but for mankind itself. Elf-maidens were the guardians of the earth, starlight and forest. It is for this reason that the elves have been called the 'Shining Ones", because they led the way.

Fairies are particularly associated with Ireland, where the ancient people of the Tuatha De Danann epitomize them. This formidable king tribe was, nevertheless, mythologized by the Christian monks, who rewrote the majority of Irish history to suit their own Church's vested interest in Ireland. From a base of the monastic texts, which arose onwards from medieval times, it is generally stated that these people were the supernatural tribe of the pre-Achaean agricultural Goddess Danae of Argos, or perhaps of the Aegean Mother-goddess Danu. But their true name, rendered in its older form, was Tuadhe d'Anu. As such, they were the people (tribe) of Anu, the great sky god of the Anunnaki. Once again we see that this fairy bloodline can be traced back thousands of years to ancient Sumer and Babylon and the god Anu. We will read more about Anu later in this chapter.

The Tuadhe d'Anu originally came from the Central European lands of Scythia, the Black Sea kingdoms which stretched from the Carpathian Mountains and Transylvanian Alps, across to the Russian River Don. They were known as the Royal Scyths and were masters of transcendent intellect.

The Tuadhe d'Anu was one of the world's most noble races and they paralleled the early noble dynastic pharaohs of Egypt. It was as a result of these Scythian-Egyptian marriages between these two families that that the Scots Gaels of Ireland came to be. It was common practice in ancient Egypt for pharaohs to marry their sisters for the sole purpose to progress their claim to kingship through the female line.

In Ancient Egypt the system for becoming a Pharaoh or ruler of the land was exclusively through heredity that is by the matrilineal royal bloodline. The Pharaoh was always male, being the oldest male heir of the previous Pharaoh. In order to rule, he had to marry a female who carried royal blood. In practical terms this meant that Pharaohs were married to their own sisters, or at least half sisters, most of the time. If a sister or half sister was unavailable, they married someone else who carried royal blood.

These wives were often half-sisters, born of their mothers by different fathers, for it was the mitochondria DNA of the matrilineal succession that was important to the dynasties. Note that both sons and daughters inherit the mitochondria from mothers, since the DNA resides within the female egg cells.

Genealogical charts of the era show that there were many successive kingly dynasties. When a pharaoh died it was important that his queen had a female heiress, because it was upon the daughter's marriage into another male line that the dynasty began. Pharaohs chose their wives very carefully, and often strategically chose to marry into more than more than one of the original Mesopotamian royal bloodline.

Occasionally the Elf-Maiden would marry a brother to solidify her claim to the throne. Cleopatra came to power in Egypt at the age of 17 by marrying her younger brother. Queen Cleopatra reigned from 51-30 BCE. It is interesting to note that the last of the pharaohs was not only a woman she was also not Egyptian. As a Ptolemy, Cleopatra was Macedonian, but even though her ancestry was not Egyptian, her royal blood ensured that this queen would be worshipped as a god.

As mentioned earlier this matrilineal royal blood can be traced back thousand of years to ancient Sumer/Babylon and to the great Anunnaki god Anu. Known as the Lord of the Sky, Anu's family line is well documented on both clay tablets and cylinder seals, dating back to 4000 BCE. This important record lists his queenly consorts as his two sisters Antu, Lady of the Sky and Ki, the Earth Mother. Anu also had two sons: Enlil, whose mother was Ki, and Enki, whose mother was Antu. Enki had two wives and one of them was his half-sister Nin-khursag, the 'Lady of Life.' Similarly, Enlil also had two wives including Nin-khursag. Therefore Nin-khursag was consort to both of her brothers.

Illustration of the Coptic Sophia, an Elf-Queen.

The rule of kingly descent through the senior female line appears to have been established from the outset when a dispute over entitlement arose between the brothers Enki and Enlil. One day, Anu, the president of the 'Grand Assembly' resigned and appointed his elder son Enlil to take his place. His brother Enki challenged his father's choice explaining that although he was younger than Enlil, he was the senior son and closer to royal succession because his mother, Anut, was Anu's senior sister, whereas Enlil's mother Ki, was Antu's junior. Therefore Enki claimed, "I am the great brother of the Gods. I am he who was born as the first son of the divine Anu." As such, it was his mother Antu who held the primary office of queen ship, and among her variously recorded titles, the later Kassite Kings of Mesopotamia called her the Lady of the Fire-stone, granting her the name Barat-Anna.

The Anunnaki overlords were said to have governed by way of a 'Grand Assembly' of nine councilors who sat at Nippur. The nine consisted of eight members (seven males and a female), who held the Rings of divine justice, along with their president, Anu, who held the One Ring to bind them all. Not only does this conform with the nine kingdoms of the Volsunga Saga, which cites Odin (Wotan) as the ultimate presidential Ring Lord, but it is also commensurate with the seven archangels of Hebraic record along with their two supervisors, the Lord of the Spirits and the Most High (equivalent to Anu). As the original God-kings of Mesopotamia, this Assembly was said to have introduced kingly practice, which, according to the Sumerian King List was 'lowered from heaven.' …

There are scattered stories about the Knight's Templar that hint that the Sinclair clan hid a sacred treasure on Oak Island, Nova Scotia, Canada. The treasure may well be the evidence that the royal bloodline, from the arrival of the Sumerians through King David to Jesus, survived the Crucifixion and is somehow alive and intact in France or Scotland. This theory may damn the Catholic Church, which claims to be structured on rigid truths. It could be seen as evidence that the Arian concept of Jesus-as-man is more correct than the Roman Church's view of him as divine. Arius was a religious man who lived between 318-355 AD. He claimed that Jesus was mortal and was not the Son of God. …

The Holy Grail itself may be a literary device for the vessel that carried the blood, or the bloodline, of Jesus. One Grail romance depicts Joseph of Arimathea as the man who brought the Grail to safety. Could Mary Magdalene have been the vessel herself, carrying the child of the martyred Messiah?

Could the Grail be an allegory for the sacred bloodline of Jesus? The central thesis of Holy Blood, Holy Grail is that the 'sangreal' or Sang Real is the Blood Royal of the family of David. The Davidic kingship extended through the generations to Jesus and on through his wife, Mary Magdalene, to the descendants exiled in Roman Gaul. The family of Jesus was assimilated into Visigothic culture and in turn into the Merovingian dynasty, whose kings went out of their way to marry Visigothic princesses to continue their own line and merge the family with the family of the Davidic line.

If we interpret the Holy Grail as the sacred bloodline, the Grail itself may comprise the documents, the written genealogies of the David-Jesus family. Robert de Boron, introduced in the 12th century, the genealogy of Percival, which extended from Joseph of Arimathea. De Boron is suspected of having been a tool for the Prieure de Sion to create legitimacy in their own kings as inheritors of the sacred bloodline.

The Prieure de Sion, or Priory of Zion, is said to be the cabal behind many of the events that occurred at Rennes-le-Chateau. According to the Prieure's own documents, its history is long and convoluted. Its earliest roots are in some sort of Hermetic or Gnostic society led by a man named Ormus. This individual is said to have reconciled paganism and Christianity. The story of Sion only comes into focus in the Middle Ages. In 1070, a group of monks from Calabria, Italy, led by one Prince Ursus, founded the Abbey of Orval in France near Stenay, in the Ardennes.

Rennes-le-Chateau is a sleepy little village located on a hilltop in the French Pyrenees. It is also home to a 9th century church, which has been restored to 19th century elegance. This church is the corner stone of one of the world's greatest mysteries and was recently featured in the best selling novel by Dan Brown, *The Da Vinci Code*.

Rennes-le-Chateau is only a short distance from the Mediterranean and popular trading routes. Many settled here while others visited and fugitives hid valuables. Why treasures were buried and why their owners never returned to claim them is an unanswered question. Pilgrims rested here before beginning the strenuous trek through the mountain crossing on their way to Compostella in Spain. The valley of the Aude hides many secrets and the land abounds with legends of hidden treasure.

It is believed that its parish priest, abbé Bérenger Saunière, discovered a treasure during the 1880s and 1890s. The treasure was large enough that he not only renovated the church but also built a villa, complete with formal garden, a belvedere and a neo-gothic tower surrounded by restored medieval ramparts.

The Priory of Sion, a European secret society founded in 1099, is allegedly a real organization. In 1975 Paris' Bibliotheque Nationale discovered parchments known as Les Dossiers Secrets, identifying members of the Priory of Sion, including Sir Isaac Newton, Botticelli, Victor Hugo and Leonardo da Vinci.

The most famous Grail romance is entitled Parzival and was written sometime between 1195 and 1216. The author was Wolfram von Eschenbach, a Bavarian knight. In his tale, Wolfram tells us about a heathen by the name of Flegetanis who is scholarly. He is descended from Solomon, and was an Israelite until he was baptized. The origin of the story apparently comes from Toledo, Spain, which was the Judaic and Muslim center for esoteric studies. Flegetanis said that while watching the constellations he could see how man's affairs and destiny were connected. He also saw what he called the Grail and said that it was left on earth by angels.

Since that time only baptized men who were chaste were allowed to guarded it.

This tale, when taken with all the information already presented, including the arrival of the Anunnaki, the lowering of kingship from heaven, and the struggle to maintain the royal blood, begs the question—why was a story about the Grail being told by a baptized Israelite? Why was this story made available to infidels when Christians were unaware of its existence?

We have always been told that the Grail Quest was a tale about finding the chalice of Jesus, or of finding the blood of Jesus. What if this assumption is wrong? Perhaps the Grail Quest is a Ring Quest: maintain the purity of the royal bloodline of the original kings and queens. The bloodline began with Adam, continued to David and was passed on to Jesus, always through the female of the family.

In *The Lord of the Rings, Cinderella, Snow White* and *Robin Hood* we see examples of the male and female royal bloodline heirs fighting dragons, defeating wicked witches or leading armies against dark lords, all for the purpose of continuing the purity of the bloodlines by seeking out their royal counterpart.

Tolkien may well have known the secret about the royal bloodline—the Sang Real. He warns us about diluting the royal blood: but in the wearing of the swift years of Middle-earth, the line of Meneldil son of Anaron failed, and the tree withered, and blood of the Numenoreans became mingled with that of lesser men.

The following is an example of a popular fairy tale: Rapunzel. Although, only an annotated version of the original tale from Jacob and Wilhelm Grimm, you should be able to see the grail message hidden in the details of the story.

Once upon a time a husband and his wife were very unhappy because they had no children. These were good people who had a little window at the back of their house, which overlooked a beautiful garden that was filled with all sorts of fragrant flowers and delicious vegetables. The problem was this garden was surrounded by a high wall and belonged to a great witch who was feared by all.

One day the woman stood at the window staring out at the garden and saw a bed full of the finest rampion: the leaves looked so delicious and fresh that she longed to eat them. This desire grew and although she knew it was wrong, she couldn't deny her want and despaired. Her husband asked:

"What ails you, dear wife?"

"Oh," she answered, "if I don't get some rampion to eat, I know I'll die."

The man realized he had to get his wife some rampion. He really didn't believe his wife would die but he knew she would continue to complain until she got the herb. So, as night began to fall, he climbed over the wall into the witch's garden, quickly harvesting a bunch of rampion and returned to his wife with her edible bouquet.

She quickly made a rampion salad, which tasted so good, instead of being satiated, she wanted more. The husband knew that if he were to get any peace at all, he had to get his wife more rampion. So once again he went over the wall and landed in the garden, He was shocked to be standing in front of the witch.

"How dare you," she said, accusingly, "climb into my garden and steal my rampion like a common thief? You shall suffer for your foolhardiness."

"Oh!" he implored, "pardon my presumption; necessity alone drove me to the deed. My wife saw your rampion from her window, and conceived such a desire for it that she would certainly have died if her wish had not been gratified." The husband's answer flattered the old witch. She spoke to him:

"If it's as you say, you may take as much rampion away with you as you like, but on one condition only: that you give me the child that your wife will shortly bring into the world. All shall go well with the child, and I will look after it like a mother."

The man, in fear for his life, acquiesced to the witch and quickly returned to his wife with the rampion. A healthy baby was born and the witch appeared to claim the child, which the witch had named Rapunzel, which meant "rampion."

Rapunzel was a very beautiful child. When she was twelve years old the Witch locked her up in a tower that had neither stairs nor doors and only had a small window near the top. When the old witch wanted to visit she stood underneath and called out: "Rapunzel, Rapunzel, Let down your golden hair."

Rapunzel had wonderful long hair, and it was as fine as spun gold. Whenever she heard the Witch's voice she unloosed her plaits, and let her hair fall down out of the window about twenty yards below, and the old Witch climbed up by it.

After they had lived like this for a few years, it happened one day that a Prince was riding through the wood and passed by the tower. As he drew near it he heard someone singing so sweetly that he stood still spellbound, and listened. It was Rapunzel in her loneliness trying to while away the time by letting her sweet voice ring out into the wood. The Prince longed to see the owner of the voice, but he sought in vain for a door in the tower. He rode home, but he was so haunted by the song he had heard that he returned every day to the wood and listened. One day, when he was standing thus behind a tree, he saw the old Witch approach and heard her call out:

"Rapunzel, Rapunzel, Let down your golden hair."

Then Rapunzel let down her plaits, and the Witch climbed up by them.

"So that's the staircase, is it?" said the Prince. "Then I too will climb it and try my luck."

So on the following day, at dusk, he went to the foot of the tower and cried:

"Rapunzel, Rapunzel. Let down your golden hair." As soon as she had let it down the Prince climbed up.

At first Rapunzel was terribly frightened when a man came in, for she had never seen one before; the Prince spoke to her so kindly, and told her at once that his heart had been so touched by her singing, that he felt he should know no peace of mind till he had seen her. Very soon Rapunzel forgot her fear, and when he asked her to marry him she consented at once. *"For,"* she thought, *"he is young and handsome, and I'll certainly be happier with him than with the old Witch."* So she put her hand in his and said: "Yes, I will gladly go with you, only how am I to get down out of the tower? Every time you come to see me you must bring a skein of silk with you, and I will make a ladder and when it is finished I will use it to climb down. Then you can take me away on your horse."

They arranged that until the ladder was ready he would visit her in the evening. The witch always visited Rapunzel during the day and never suspected anything. One day, Rapunzel commented, without thinking, "How is it, good mother, that you are so much harder to pull up than the young Prince? He is always with me in a moment."

"Oh! you wicked child," cried the Witch. "What is this I hear? I thought I had hidden you safely from the whole world, and in spite of it you have managed to deceive me."

Filled with rage the Witch grabbed Rapunzel's hair and wound it round her left hand, and then seizing a pair of scissors sliced Rapunzel's beautiful plaits clean off and watched as they fell to the ground. Then, the old Witch dragged Rapunzel and hid her in a deserted place, where she would be lonely and miserable.

The young prince not knowing of the day's events approached the tower and looking up to the open window whispered:

"Rapunzel, Rapunzel, Let down your golden hair."

The golden hair plummeted down, taking it his strong hands the prince climbed higher and higher and lifted himself through the window. He turned to look at Rapunzel and was horrified to see the old Witch starring at him with contemptuous eyes. She said sarcastically:

"Ah, ah! you thought to find your ladylove, but the pretty bird has flown and its song is dumb; the cat caught it, and will scratch out your eyes too. Rapunzel is lost to you for ever—you will never see her more."

The Prince fearing for his life jumped out of the window to escape. He landed safely but was blinded by thorns that twisted round the tower.

He wandered aimlessly through unfamiliar woods, eating nothing but roots and berries. Tears swelled up in his sightless eyes as he stumbled forward lamenting his lost love. One day he was walking in the forest and heard Rapunzel singing. He found her alone with their two children.

Healed, he led her to his kingdom, where they were received and welcomed with great joy, and they lived happily ever after. And what is the hidden message behind this story. Basically, Rapunzel is an Elf-maiden of the royal bloodline and she has been locked away and hidden in a tower from her prince, an Elf-prince also of the royal bloodline. To perpetuate the royal bloodline they must meet, they must mate regardless of the obstacles. Why were they separated? Why was there suddenly such desperation on behalf of the royals to wed and to mate? The answer is in the next chapter.

19

Donation of Constantine

Aragorn was the son of Arathorn, and he knew his destiny was that as the ruler of the Dunedian. He was simply a king in exile at the time of The Lord of the Rings. His royal blood was mixed with that of Elvin blood and traced back to the beginning of Middle-earth. Even as Strider, he realized his duty was to fiercely resist the Dark Lord and the servants of Mordor. Tolkien has written about the importance of the royal bloodline and how the people of Middle-earth knew it, and how important it was to their lives.

The 'Royal Bloodline' was successfully handed down from generation to generation and was unanimously accepted by people, either common or gentry. Even the Church recognized the importance of the heritage of the royal bloodline, in establishing and maintaining the foundation of civilization.

This royal bloodline (Sang Real) was always passed down through the female of the family. The matrilineal heritage of the royal bloodline included the Biblical figures of Lilith, Miriam, Bathsheba and Mary Magdalene.

That was until an obscure document, alleged to have been written by Constantine, was unearthed, from which we highlight here: the chief Roman ecclesiastics, among whom senators may also be received, shall obtain the same honors and distinctions as the senators. Like the emperor the Roman Church shall have as functionaries, cubicularii, ostiarii, and excubitores. The pope shall enjoy the same honorary rights as the emperor, among them the right to wear an imperial crown, a purple cloak and tunic, and in general all imperial insignia or signs of distinction.

The pope was also to be given the service of a strator that was a man to lead the horse upon which the pope rode. Moreover, the emperor makes a present to the pope and his successors of the Lateran palace, of Rome and the provinces, districts, and towns of Italy and all the Western regions (tam palatium nostrum, ut prelatum est, quamque Romæ urbis et omnes Italiæ seu occidentalium regionum provinicas loca et civitates). The pope was to rule over the whole West to the

Vicar of Christ. All kings in Western Europe were thus nothing more than tenants of the pope's land, and their positions had to be ratified by him.

The Donation of Constantine came to prominence when Charles Martel died in 741. Charles Martel was one of most heroic figures in French history. He led the French army against the Moorish invasion of France at the Battle of Tours-Poitiers in 732. From 711 A.D. Muslim forces crossed the Straits of Gibraltar, conquered the Visigothic Kingdom. Spain lay under Arab control. In less than ten years, the Arabs crossed the Pyrenees. In 732, under the command of Abd-er-rahman, Charles Martel, and the Franks at the Battle of Poitiers also known as the battle of Tours decisively defeated them. This battle looms large in our Western history.

Charles Martel's son Pepin III, who was the Mayor of the Palace to King Childeric III, who was the last Merovingian king, petitioned the Church to support his bid for the crown.

The Church decided that its best political move was to support Pepin III's claim for the crown, in spite of the fact that this support would undermine its promise to the Merovingian family. By apostolic authority the Pope ordered that Pepin be created King of the Franks. Pepin then confined the king to a monastery where he died four years later.

The document that allowed the pope to choose Pepin over Childeric III states that Constantine gave the bishop of Rome his imperial symbols and regalia. It also states that for the first time the document named the bishop of Rome as the "Vicar of Christ." Apparently, the bishop of Rome returned the imperial symbols and regalia to Constantine who wore them with ecclesiastical (the Church) sanction.

According to the 'Donation of Constantine' the bishop of Rome now had the authority, through Constantine, to not only be the supreme spiritual authority over Christendom, but also became the supreme secular power in Christendom. In other words, the bishop of Rome, the pope became a papal emperor, with the power to choose and then anoint kings.

When Pepin was crowned king, bishops, for the first time, were allowed to attend the ceremony. Also, they were now regarded not only as clergy, but now had rank equal to that of secular (worldly rather than spiritual) noble. The Church no longer was bound to recognize a king, through his royal blood, but now by power of the document could create kingship.

It was almost as if the bishop of Rome had the magical power bestowed by God through Constantine to alter the genetic makeup of the new king's blood to create a new "Church Blessed' royal bloodline! Anointing of a king became little more than a symbolic gesture of conferring divine grace upon a ruler. Indeed, now Holy oil replaced the Sang Real.

Interestedly, the coronation of Pepin III was the beginning of one of the most powerful families in Europe and led directly to the Carolingian dynasty. Most people believe that Charles the Great—Charlemagne—was the genesis of the Carolingians, but the actual founder was Charles Martel.

Charlemagne was by far the most famous Carolingian. He not only became king but was also proclaimed as the Holy Roman Emperor in 800 AD. Traditionally and historically, the title should have been reserved exclusively for someone of the Merovingian bloodline because they were the carriers of the Sang Real.

Charlemagne, although loyal to the Roman Church, realized the importance of the royal bloodline, and indeed was somewhat entitled to his position because his maternal grandmother was Merovingian. He also knew that his father, appointed by the Church, was thought to be a usurper. Therefore, Charlemagne believed he held his office by papal decree only. He also knew that kingship was carried in the matrilineal blood (the mitochondria DNA) of the female line and his half-sister Berthelde married into the Pict-sidhe strain, which had even more seniority than the Merovingian. This fact alone guaranteed acceptance of the Carolingian line of monarchs.

As mentioned earlier the Church had pledged itself to the Merovingian bloodline in 496. It was only the Donation of Constantine that allowed the Church to betray its recognition of the true royal blood.

The Donation of Constantine made its first appearance in the 8th century, some 400 years after Constantine purportedly wrote it. Where it had been hidden or preserved for this interim period is anybody's guess. By its very discovery all monastic and civic authority in Europe, has been transferred to families that the Church handpicked, rather than those of the royal bloodline.

The document is apparently signed and dated by Emperor Constantine; however, this document is fraudulent. The opening and closing sections of the Donation were written in the style characteristic of Constantine's day. But, its contents appear to be inconsistent with history. At one point the city of Constantinople is referenced as being in existence and at another point its creation is being planned for the future. Finally, the 15th century linguist Lorenzo Valla declared that the document was an outright forgery. For centuries the document was the sole basis for papal territorial and jurisdictional claims in Europe. The first draft of the document was likely created in the later part of the 8th century. It was created to assist Pope Stephen II in his negotiations with the Frankish Mayor of the Palace, Pepin III. The Pope crossed the Alps to anoint him as king in 754. Pepin III was a member of the Carolingian family. In return, he seems to have promised to give to the Pope those lands in Italy, which the Lombards had taken from Byzantium. The promise was fulfilled in 756. Constantine's alleged gift made it possible to interpret Pepin's grant not as a benefaction but as a restoration.

One of the greatest threats facing the Roman Church before 751 was the Merovingian family. As mentioned earlier, the Merovingian bloodline can be traced back to the family of Jesus. The Merovingian kings, by their right as carriers of the royal bloodline, passed kingship from generation to generation, and were truly servants of their people.

When Childeric died in 481, his successor was his son Clovis. At that time the Roman Church was not the most prominent religion in Europe. Arianism was threatening their claim to be the Church. Arianism was a religion that claimed that Jesus Christ and God the Father were not essentially one and the same. The Arians believed that the God created the son and therefore lower in importance. Some Arians also believed that Jesus was a prophet. This belief was so prominent that for a time Arianism was more popular that Christianity.

The Church hoped that Clovis, being neither Catholic nor Arian, could assist them. It also was helpful that Clovis married Burgundian Princess Clotilde, who was a devote Catholic and openly evangelized her faith.

King Clovis and his army were engaged in a battle near Cologne with an invading army of Alamanni tribesman. When it appeared that his army would be defeated Clovis invoked the name of Jesus Christ and the tide of war changed. Subsequently, Clovis gave thanks to the victory, at least in part, to Jesus Christ. His wife on hearing the news sent for the Catholic Bishop of Reims who immediately baptized him.

Many of Clovis' warriors soon converted to the Roman Church and its prominence as the leading Christian religion in Europe was assured.

The Church in gratitude promised the Merovingian perpetual allegiance, and it was this allegiance that they broke when they allowed Pepin III to be crowned king.

Thousands of years earlier, the Nephilim requested that the Anunnaki create a position that would be an intermediary between themselves and humans. The Nephilim thought of themselves as overlords and since the creation of mankind the entire Anunnaki hierarchy had changed. No longer were the Nephilim simply laborers: working in the gold mines or harvesting crops. Now Mankind labored and the Nephilim oversaw and managed. It was decided by the council that kingship should be lowered to earth and bestowed on a human. This human ruler would guarantee Mankind's service to the Gods and communicate the teachings and laws of the Gods to the people.

As previously mentioned, many of the Nephilim had married human woman and had children by them. It was out of these children that the Nephilim/Anunnaki chose their first human kings. These demigods, these kings were entrusted with the care of well being of their people and as proof of this obligation carried the royal scepter as well as a shepherd's crook.

What real importance does this have? Originally, the royal bloodline, and kingship through the bloodline, was lowered from heaven and that the kings were servants of the Gods entrusted with the administration of divine laws of justice. By virtue of the fact that the Church took over the ordination of kings, transplanting the original authority of the kings' royal bloodline, the kings themselves became servants of the Church, instead of servants of the people.

Once again we are presented with the date of 4000 BCE. This date coincides with the creation of Sumer according to ancient cylinder seals and to the creation by God of Adam and Eve. Coincidently, Tolkien for *The Lord Of The Rings* also cites the time period.

Why is this date so important to this book? It is because this date was the starting point from which kingship was bestowed on earth, and from which the royal blood, resulting from gods mating with humans, began to be passed genetically from generation to generation through the female's maternal DNA. It was the importance of maintaining the purity and the sanctity of this blood, this Sang Real, that caused the creation of the 'Grail Quest,' when the Church, citing the authority of the Donation of Constantine, decided that it only had the power to bestow kingship on earth and that hereditary kingship was forbidden and that those loyal to bloodline were deemed by the Church as heretics.

20

Of Dragons and Giant Eagles

Artist's drawing of a Dragon.

Tolkien writes that dragons were among the most feared of the servants of the Dark Lord. The first dragon was Glaurung, the Father of Dragons, and he lived in the middle of the First Age. Following Glaurung many other dragons came and harassed both Elves and Men. Among them the infamous dragons were Ancalagon the first winged dragon, Scatha who dwelt in the cold northern wastes and Smaug who was the last of the great dragons and guarded treasure in *The Hobbit*.

The dragons were not destroyed at the end of the Third Age; and some believe that they have survived to our own time. In *The Hobbit*, Bilbo is recruited to help some dwarves steal back their treasure that was originally stolen by the dragon Smaug in the Lonely Mountain.

Bilbo finds the courage to enter the dragon's lair and steals a golden cup. Smaug wakes up and in retaliation kills their ponies. Bilbo reenters the lair and has a conversation with the dragon and discovers that the dragon has a weak spot over its left breast. This eventually leads to Smaug's death and the recovery of the treasure.

In *The Lord of the Rings* the Ringwraiths, the Nazgûl rode dragons while searching for Frodo.

In the movie Excalibur, the magician Merlin described dragons to a young King Arthur, "The dragon, a beast of such power, that if you were to see it whole, and all complete in one single glance, it would burn you to cinders ..." What is the truth about dragons? Are they the stuff of fairy tales or are they as many believe real animals that may exist even today.

It was only a thousand years ago that dragons were the subjects of gossip and everyone from kings, bishops and stable boys knew of their individual characteristics and descriptions. Dragon graffiti painted the walls of Medieval Europe. Children aspired to being dragon slayers as much as they dreamed of being knights. Becoming a dragon slayer was a genuine occupation. It was a guaranteed way to get the girls and the money, if you lived.

Knights, saints and other brave souls routinely killed dragons that terrorized towns and villages. From Europe to China tales of dragons were as common as the gossip of today's movie stars and celebrities.

One of the most famous dragon tales involves St. George who was born in Cappadocia (now Eastern Turkey) in the year 270 AD. He was a Christian and at the age of seventeen joined the Roman army and soon distinguished himself by his bravery.

He was sent to England and gathered much notoriety by protecting Christians that were to be tortured by his fellow Romans.

While he was in England he heard the Emperor was putting all Christians to death and so he returned to Rome to help. He pleaded with the Emperor Diocletian to spare their lives but could not persuade him. St. George was ordered to give up his faith. He refused and was beheaded on April 23, 303.

On one of St. George's journeys he came to Libya. There he a met a hermit that told him the cause of the great sorrow that had fallen over the land. Apparently a dragon was ravaging the country.

The cost to appease the dragon was the daily sacrifice of a beautiful maiden. But now, all the young girls have been killed and only the King's daughter remained.

The King promised his daughter in marriage to anyone that could slay the dragon. As any heroic knight would do St. George vowed that he would destroy the monster.

The next day, St. George rose early, and traveled to where the sacrifices took place. There he saw a beautiful girl dressed in pure Arabian silk. It was the princess and her name was Sabra. He told her and her entourage that he would slay the dragon and she was to return to the palace.

He then entered the valley where the dragon lived. Suddenly the dragon, which had a huge head and a tail that was fifty feet long, rushed from its cave and St. George charged and struck the dragon with his spear. It smashed into a thousand pieces and he was thrown to the ground.

Recovering quickly, he got to his feet and drew his sword. The dragon was ready and spit poison over him which split his armor in two. He staggered away and fell under an enchanted orange tree, which miraculously rejuvenated him. Rising again with sword in hand he rushed the dragon and stabbed it under the wing where there were no scales. It fell dead at his feet.

Dragons were not the stuff of myths and children's tales, but the subject of newsworthiness. Kings, knights, monks, archbishops and scholars reported eyewitness accounts of these events.

Sir John Mandeville in his medieval work *Travels*, written approximately 1366, chronicles his voyages to the East. As an English knight who left England around 1322 he journeyed to Egypt, Ethiopia, India, Persia, and Turkey. He describes the Tower of Babylon as being "… full of dragons and great serpents, and full of dyverse venymous beasts all about." Today, it is commonly accepted that Sir John did not write *Travels*, as it was the practice of unknown writers to credit well-known individuals in hopes of gaining monetarily from their efforts. *Travels* was certainly one of the most popular books of the late Middle Ages, indeed hundreds of medieval manuscript copies of it have survived to the present day.

Dragons were also the subjects of controversy. Scholarly debates would occasionally climax in all out brawls when one side would insist that dragons had their offspring by laying eggs and the other side would argue that dragons gave birth to their young like mammals. The monetary cost of having a dragon dwelling nearby was financially devastating to the community. It was said the appetite of a dragon was such that one could devour countless cattle, sheep and maidens. There is a report that Pope St. Sylvester kept a dragon and that it eat 6000 people a day.

There is a fresco, painted by Italian painter Maso Di Banco circa 1340 that depicts a scene known as the "dragon miracle" set in Rome in the ruins of the Forum Romanum. It shows Pope Sylvester putting chains on a dragon then turning to the dead Magi and raising him from the dead. Emperor Constantine and his companions look on in astonishment.

So heavy was the demand for dragons among European alchemists and among Ethiopians that a minor trade war erupted in the 13th century. Dragon meat was a delicacy to Ethiopians.

Inevitably, the growing demand for dragons and their derivatives led to commercial conflict. In the 13th century, Friar Roger Bacon complained that "it is certain" that Ethiopian sages were coming to Europe, to "those Christian lands where there are good flying dragons," and luring dragons from their caves, saddling them, and then riding them back to Ethiopia where they would be butchered and eaten. A century later, European merchants, having belatedly grasped the commercial possibilities of the dragon trade, had established their own agents locally to acquire dragons for export to Ethiopia. It can be assumed that they advertised European dragons as a superior breed, and charged accordingly. And thus the systematic slaughter of dragons began, and decimated their numbers in both Europe and Africa.

For those that believe that this is just an ordinary friar reporting this, note that Friar Roger Bacon was a true science pioneer and admirer of Thomas Aquinas. Bacon is famous for stating, "Mathematics is the door and the key to the science". He came to the conclusion that one of the best ways to verify one's theories was to test them through experiment. In thirteenth century Europe the Roman Church didn't eagerly accept experimental evidence. Church doctrine dictated that the power of reason could only be used as a tool when equally infused with the wisdom of God. The Church was the absolute authority on all things, scientific or not. The Inquisition punished those with new scientific ideas with imprisonment, torture or death. 8

One of the earliest works of English literature is the classic tale of Beowulf. It is one of the most valuable single treasures of English literary history and today is housed in the British Museum. One of the main characters of this poem is the dragon Grendel. He is described as being a fiend of hell and a monster grim. 9

Speaking of bad press, the above paints a rather poor picture of the dragon Grendel. I would rather think of dragons as the one that was portrayed in the movie Dragon Heart with Sean Connery's English accent and sense of humor. Another movie classic featuring a very aerodynamic dragon was *Dragonslayer*.

Ok, but what do we know about the origins of dragons? Believe it or not the same clay tablets and copper seals that tell us so much about the Sumerians and the origins of the Christian and Jewish Bibles, tell us also about the birth of dragons! Seven clay tablets that were unearthed by archeologists form a single narrative known as the Babylonian Creation Epic. It describes how the Gods were born and man created.

As in the Bible, it starts, "In the beginning …" and states that there were neither land, Gods nor men, and that only two things existed: Apsu and Tiamat. Apsu was male and represented fresh water and the void in which the world would be created. Tiamat was female and was the opposite of Apsu. She represented salt water as well as chaos. Some say the battle of the sexes has been going on since the beginning of time. The descriptions of Apsu and Tiamat would certainly support that contention! Tiamat is described as being like a monster with a serpentine body complete with scales, legs and horns protruding from her head. She is known as the first dragon of history! No description of Apsu is available. 10

Dragon or not, she and Apsu mated and had an odd assortment of offspring. These children grew up to become the new Gods of earth. They were apparently unruly and disrespectful to the parents; causing Apsu to complain to Tiamat, Apsu claimed that the children were loathsome. They bothered him constantly; preventing him from getting any rest. Sounds pretty much like a typical family; children running amok and parents stressed to the limit. Still, Apsu's solution was a bit drastic. He planned to murder his children!

Tiamat begged Apsu to reconsider and not to destroy their children. Somehow, the children learned of their father's plans and struck first. They attacked him, bound him and then murdered him. Tiamat was distraught by the treachery of her children and could not be consoled. Her offspring were as defiant as ever, so to avenge her husband, she gave birth to a second brood of children. Since, Apsu was dead, I can only assume the pregnancy was divine intervention.

Anyway, in time she gave birth to a ferocious assortment of devils: giant serpents, roaring dragons, lion-demons, scorpion-men and the centaur!

Her original children decided that a fight to the death with their mother and her new brood would not benefit them. After seeing them, the original children realized that their new siblings were a virtually undefeatable army and that any confrontation with them would be disastrous.

Another plan had to be implemented. They had to convince one of their own to fight their mother in single combat! One of the children stepped forward and accepted the challenge of combat with his mother. His name was Marduk and he only had one condition. If he was victorious in combat he was to be recognized and acknowledged by his brethren as king of the universe! His immediate family accepted.

The combat began and as all good storytellers describe … it was an epic struggle! Marduk was victorious and slew his mother. He had a magic net, in which he captured all of Tiamat's new brood, and he killed them without hesitation. He also was rewarded with the Tablets of Destiny, which were found hidden in one of the offspring's bodies.

As the new God of the universe, Marduk created both the heavens and earth. As you may remember, Marduk has been mentioned earlier in this book. He was the king of Babylon. In this retelling of the creation myth, Marduk's name replaces that of AN, supreme God of the Anunnaki.

There are unexplored regions of the earth that still may be home to dragons today. Reports from China tell of eyewitnesses who had been present at various dragon sightings. In 1944 a black dragon suddenly fell from the sky crashing to the ground in the Chen Family's Weizi Village in Heilongjiange province. 11

The dragon was very ill and near death. It was described as being covered with scales and had a horn protruding from its head. There may also be photographic proof of dragons!

In June 22, 2004, an amateur photographer shot a picture from an airplane flying over the Himalayas Mountains. It appears to show two dragons in flight. Although, the photographer didn't capture the entire bodies of the creatures in-frame, what we see is quite amazing and thought provoking. 12

Captured are conical bodies, tapering to what we can imagine are tails. Reptilian looking scales are clearly present and what's most remarkable about the objects is that they appear to be in-flight, high above the actual mountains.

In June 22, 2004, an amateur photographer shot a picture from an airplane flying over the Himalayas Mountains. It appears to show two dragons in flight. Although, the photographer didn't capture the entire bodies of the creatures in-frame, what we see is quite amazing and thought provoking.

Haast Giant Eagle

But what about Tolkien's giant eagles: is there proof of gigantic birds in our past and if so, are they still here?

According to the BBC News—UK Edition, the giant eagles that swooped down to rescue Sam and Frodo in JRR Tolkien's The Lord of the Rings had a real counterpart. http://news.bbc.co.uk/1/hi/sci/tech/4138147.stm

The giant eagle was one of the largest birds of prey ever recorded and was once New Zealand's chief predator, DNA evidence from fossil bones indicates. The image of giant eagles flying around New Zealand, while fanciful, is not so far-fetched as it might appear, scientists say.

New research was published in the journal PLoS Biology that claims that the bird, named Haast's eagle, was the island's major predator.

It increased its weight at an incredible rate unparalleled by other birds or animals. Unfortunately, the giant eagle became extinct approximately 500 years ago, 200 years after the arrival of man. Coincidently, the giant eagles main food source the moa also died out 500 years ago. New Zealand was home to several species of moa, a flightless bird ranging in height from less than two feet to more than six feet tall and weighing from 45 to 550 pounds.

Evidence of eagle attacks remain, as holes and rents torn into the bones of moa, which show that the eagle struck from the side, gripped the moa's pelvic area with one foot, and killed with a single strike by the other foot to the neck or head. The eagle is thought to be the bird called "Hokioi" in the oral history of the Maori, a native people. Its existence is recorded in rock art, and artifacts shaped from eagle bone prove that the bird co-existed with early Polynesians, according to researchers. However, there is no evidence that humans were targets for this huge aerial predator.

The research is the work of scientists from the universities of Oxford, UK, and Canterbury, New Zealand.

The researchers, led by Professor Alan Cooper from Oxford's Ancient Biomolecules Centre, extracted DNA from fossil eagle bones dating back about 2,000 years.

Sufficient scientific and anecdotal evidence exists that prove the possibility that perhaps both dragons and giant eagles once lived on earth. Tolkien may have reasoned that these creatures were not purely mythical and chose them to also inhabit his Middle-earth.

I live on the north shore of Lake Erie and have witnessed many strange birds flying overhead. Some seem gigantic. I normally see them through the central skylight of the cottage or glimpse them through the branches of the very tall maple trees that populate our property. These birds could be hawks, eagles or turkey vultures (buzzards) or something else. Regardless, they seem huge when soaring overhead.

Another oddity of my residence is the belief by some that the lake is the home of a lake monster. Affectionately, known as South Bay Bessie, this creature has reportedly been seen since 1817. I receive eyewitness accounts on a regular basis of what some refer to as the creature.

South Bay Bessie as we all know is not the only lake monster on the planet. Indeed, Tolkien must have been aware of the most famous or at least the most publicized lake monster, Jessie, the legendary inhabitant of Loch Ness. I traveled to the small town of Drumnadrochit, Scotland in 2002 to look for Nessie.

Drumnadrochit is on the shores of Loch Ness, just 13 miles from Inverness. It is the home of the Loch Ness Exhibition Centre and of Urquhart Castle. Many sightings have been seen at or near Urquhart Castle. I walked around the area, took one of the Loch Ness cruises and spoke to many of the residents. Thousands of people travel to Loch Ness annually, all hoping to catch a glimpse of the elusive creature. Most, like myself, leave without witnessing Nessie but still savor the memory of the Highlands and of staring into the blackness that is Loch Ness.

21

Conclusions

When I began writing this book I set out to explore the possibility that *The Lord of the Rings* was based on historical fact. I discovered that the history I was searching for was hidden in ancient myth and folklore. Many believe that myths and fairy tales were the basis for understanding our lost past. I wanted to discover if these or other factors influenced Tolkien's writings.

I did not set out to cast doubt on anyone's religious beliefs or to attack any religious organization. I did not set out to discover space aliens or little green men. I simply set out to see if our historical past reflected Tolkien's stories. To validate my hypothesis I attempted to find proof that Tolkien's Middle-earth paralleled the early years of our world. I needed to compare creation stories from around the globe to see if they had any similarities with Middle-earth.

Tolkien writes that the creator of Middle-earth was Ilúvatar. He made the world and the Ainur (angels), Elves and Man. The Valar were like Archangels and were of the Ainur. They had Godlike abilities and created the Dwarves, Orcs and other beings. They also roamed the earth and interacted with the Elves, Humans and Dwarves. They believed in the divine plan of Ilúvatar and worked in Middle-earth to accomplish it.

The evil Lord Sauron's master was Melkor, also one of Valar before he was cast out. Sauron had amazing powers and could control the dead and by will alone manipulate men and others creatures.

One could also make the argument that there are more comparisons between *The Lord of the Rings*, the Bible and history. Gandalf the Gray sacrificed himself to save his friends, members of the *Fellowship of the Ring*. He was resurrected only days later as Gandalf the White.

The description of Gandalf is fundamental to the understanding of our ancient past. Tolkien describes Gandalf in The Hobbit as being an old man with a long gray cloak and a long white beard. He has also always been portrayed as being a white man. Identical descriptions of individuals with amazing powers have been seen throughout history and throughout the world.

In Mexico the God Quelzalcoutl or Kukulkan was portrayed as being a tall white man with a long beard wearing a robe. The Indians of Peru depict Viracocha as being a tall white man, bearded, wearing a white robe that was belted at the waist.

Viracocha was a teacher. It was said that before he came to Peru, "men lived in a condition of disorder, many went naked like savages, and they had no houses or other dwellings than caves, and from these went forth to gather whatever they would find to eat in the countryside."

Ironically, the Peruvian Indians description of early man is identical to that of the Nummo who stated that man was naked and speechless. They identified this lack of intelligence as disorder. It is my opinion that the Nummo were the Anunnaki as they both settled in the Middle East and both are depicted as fish or reptilian.

Gods were the architects of great wars. Battles were fought, heroes emerged and thousands perished. Gods fought alongside men and influenced the outcome of battles. In the Battle of Troy, the Gods were not only spectators but also participants and in ancient Egypt the Metal People fought with Ra and Horus to destroy Seth! Were the aerial combats fought in the skies over Egypt the basis for the gargantuan battles fought between the Tolkien's dragons and giant eagles?

We have read that it was only one thousand years ago, that men of every level of society believed in and actually gossiped about dragons. Our teachers taught us that what these people actually saw was based on reports of the discovery of the bones of prehistoric dinosaurs. This explanation is extremely weak. We can't state definitely that dragons actually existed a millennium ago, but we can state with some certainty that eyewitness accounts were recorded and these witnesses believed that they had seen dragons.

Researchers have reported that there is proof that giant eagles actually existed only 500 years ago. In fact it was considered the major predator of its time on New Zealand!

If proof of giant eagles has been found as reported, it may only be a matter of time before proof of dragons is also confirmed! The most familiar creation story for comparison purposes is the one found in the Bible. It's similar to Tolkien's story in that there is only one God and he created the earth, angels and mankind. Lucifer is an archangel and like Melkor is cast out of heaven along with his followers.

The Bible and the Book of Enoch inform us that the angels or the Nephilim came down to earth and interacted with, even married, humans.

Biblical accounts also tell us that there were other humans on earth at the time of Adam and Eve. But that these races were not made or created in the image of God!

The main difference between the two tales is that Ilúvatar favored the Elves and God favored Man.

Throughout this book we have learned that there are still earlier creation myths than recorded in the Bible. It is these myths that form the foundation of all of our creation stories.

The earliest known comes from Sumer, which is now Iraq. It states that the Anunnaki came to earth and created Man to serve as labor to mine gold. This may explain why, throughout history, gold has always been a prized possession. The truly amazing part of these stories is in the detailed accounts, which were written down and survive even today. The story begins some 400,000 years and explains how they manipulated the DNA of Home erectus by mixing it with their own DNA to create an entirely new species; Home sapien.

Scientists have searched tirelessly for proof that man is descendent from great apes. Evolution dictates that this link be found and anthropologists have searched unsuccessfully for this evidence for hundreds of years.

In 1871, Charles Darwin coined the expression 'missing link' after he noticed an anomaly in the human evolutionary progression. There was a gap, a hole, a mystery to be filled, linking the great apes to modern man! Darwin believed that man must have evolved from a ground-dwelling ape that walked on two feet.

In November of 2004 scientists in northeast Spain discovered the 13 million-year-old remains of a tree-climbing creature, which may be the last common ancestor of modern-day great apes and humans. Experts agree that the find is simply a starting point. It is the first fossil to show characteristics of a modern great ape.

Remember Lloyd Pye's claim that great apes have 48 pairs of chromosomes and humans only 46 and that our second and third chromosomes have been fused together—perhaps proving that we were mated with a creature with only 46 chromosomes.

The Anunnaki were called the Sumerians because they dwelt in Sumer and they bestowed kingship on earth. They created Adam and he was the first priest-king and possessor of the original royal blood. They may also have created, by accident or by design, the Minotaur, Centaur, Cyclops, Gorgons, Hippocentaur and other supposedly mythical creatures. The Mermaids and Mermen of folklore may have be a creation of the Anunnaki. This species of half fish—half human may have been developed specifically to mine for gold on the ocean floor!

They were the original angels and Nephilim that were sexually attracted to the offspring of Adam and Eve. They intermarried with humans and became the mothers and fathers of the demigods of history. Their names remain in our collective consciousness as the heroes of our distant past: Achilles, Hercules, Samson and Thor to name but a few.

It was the Anunnaki that created the Elf-lords to perpetuate the royal blood and procreated dragons as in the story of Apsu and Tiamat. The love shared between Aragorn and Arwen is one of the central themes in The Lord of the Rings. It was imperative that these two lovers mated to not only continue the bloodline, but also to heal the land of Gondor that had been without a king.

So what again is the royal bloodline and what does it mean? The patriarch or the matriarch of the family always arranged family marriages. They did this to maintain the purity of the bloodline. This bloodline was the wellspring that flowed from the original Adam to King David and to Jesus and to the Kings and Queens of Europe.

There is a great deal of contention, which was captured literally in the best selling novel, The Da Vinci Code, that speculates that Jesus married Mary Magdalene and they'd one or more children? We know from historical records that Mary traveled with Jesus' uncle Joseph of Arimathea and went to France and England. Was she pregnant or did she carry a child and was this the Holy Grail? Tolkien informs us of the result of mixing or the dying off of the royal blood: "But in the wearing of the swift years of Middle-earth, the line of Meneldil son of Anaron failed, and the tree withered, and blood of the Numenoreans became mingled with that of lesser men."

Aragorn was of the royal bloodline of Meneldil and it was necessary for him to marry Arwen to solidify his position and to be recognized by the people as the rightful king.

Would it surprise you to learn that there is evidence that the races portrayed in The Lord of the Rings, not only existed but also may continue to exist today. Remember the news article in Chapter V, "The hobbit was nobody's fool," Roberts said. "They survived alongside us for at least 30,000 years, and were not known for being very amiable eco-companions. And the hobbits were managing some extraordinary things-manufacturing sophisticated stone tools, hunting pygmy elephants, and crossing at least two water barriers to reach Flores from mainland Asia-with a brain only one-third the size of ours.

Dwarves or little people have existed for thousand of years and are still present in our society today. The gene that causes their abnormality, like the royal blood, is passed from generation to generation, but rarely surfaces. Does this gene prove that Dwarves once were a race of people that inhabited earth?

Remember The Eye of Sauron, and how it caused almost constant dread for Frodo. It was as if the very stare from the eye seemed to sap him of his strength and will as he continued toward Mount Doom. The Anunnaki had their own version of Tolkien's "Eye of Sauron": it was known as the "Terrible Eye". Enlil from his city of Nippur could use beams to search and scan all the lands and Ninuta the Sumero-Babylonian God also was said to possess a terrible eye that was capable of searching and scanning the land.

The kings of our past ruled by the power of their rings and divine blood. One of the oldest ring tales is The Volsunga Saga, based on Norse mythology. This story from Iceland concerns a magical ring made of red gold that enables its owner to weave great wealth. Tolkien was aware of this saga and others concerning rings. As an Oxford University professor he was aware of ancient myths, especially the tales of the Norse God Odin, king of the Vikings. Odin is the same God as the Saxon's God Wotan. Odin was a Ring-Lord and governed as president over nine kingdoms. Each ruler of the individual kingdoms was given a ring, and it was his ring that bound all of the other rings and their wearers to him. Tolkien was so inspired by these and other myths that he learned Finnish so that he could read these stories in their original text, including The Saga of the Ring, The Kingdom of the Circle and the Kalevala.

The Kalevala, a collection of runes, has been compared to Homer's Odyssey. Storytellers known as rune singers have passed down the Kalevala through the ages. These stories of myth and magic and the entire history of the Finnish people are sung as oral history. Today, only one elderly gentleman, Jussi Houvinen, sings the runes. Fortunately, during the last century these remarkable histories have been recorded both in words and music and will continue long after Mr. Houvinen.

The Kalevala's verses with their lyrical tones of the Finnish language inspired Tolkien to give his Elves a language strikingly similar to Finnish. The Kavevala has characters and themes that may have influenced Tolkien's Middle-earth.

The Kalevala includes many mystical elements including shape-shifters, demons, magical plants and animals that can transform into humans. The story includes a quest for a sacred object of great power and once found, discovering the meaning and purpose of the object.

These tales may well have been based on still earlier stories originating with the Anunnaki of Sumer. Their Grand Assembly consisted of eight councilors: one for each kingdom or region. They were given and ruled by their rings, which were reported to be of divine power. It was Ring power that was responsible for the establishment of municipal government and kingly rule. The president of the Grand Assembly held the One Ring that bound the member councilors to the president. This is perhaps the strongest argument that I can make regarding the historical proof of Tolkien's works. His words not only resemble actual recorded history but also seem to stem from it:

One Ring to rule them all, One Ring to find them,

One Ring to bring them all and in the darkness bind them.

If you desire to discover more truth about our origins and how they relate to Tolkien's Middle-earth, read the books written by Zecharia Sitchin, Laurence Gardner, Graham Hancock, Steven Sora and Shannon Dorey.

Our educational system fails to teach the truth about our ancient beginnings. Teachers rely on the information that they were taught. Remember in the Introduction I wrote about scientists and how they'd forgotten to ask the question: What if? It is these scientists that write the textbooks that are used to teach our children today. These books, newly printed, contain the same accepted dogma that we were taught.

Organized religion has its own reason to stick to the status quo. For thousands of years Christianity, Judaism and Islam have become the largest religions in the world. They did this by relying on ancient scriptures that were based on older texts from Sumer and Babylon. These original stories were translated, updated and rewritten to reflect their biblical times. Monotheism replaced Polytheism and pagan stories about the Garden of Eden, the creation of Adam and Eve and the deluge became the foundation stones of new religions.

Emperor Constantine and his successors completely altered Christian doctrine and set up a church hierarchy with newly established beliefs and practices, which are the basis for all mainstream Bible-based churches. They accomplished this by only including books of the Bible that supported their position.

The modern Christian bible was created to support a political position from which the foundations of all Christian religions were built. Many traditional books of the Bible were not included in the Laodicea (360 AD) and subsequent councils, including the Book of Enoch, The Gospel According to Mary Magdalene and the Apocalypse of Thomas to name only three.

The one god replaced the pantheons of gods and tales of the Anunnaki were transformed into tales of the Nephilim and angels. Educate yourself by learning about your family. Discover where your parents and grand parents were born. Invest in a family tree and document the genealogy of your family. If your family is from Europe, Asia, Africa, North or South America, Australia or some other area of the world, plan a vacation there and locate any living relatives and have them tell you about their parents and grandparents. The more you learn about them the more you learn about yourself!

But if you are in a hurry to find the proof, simply look deep into your bathroom mirror and don't be surprised if Gandalf, Gimil, Legolas, Sam or Frodo smiles back.

The Quest for Middle-earth will really never end. Its story and that of other similar folktales and myths make up an essential element of our being. This search is one of the primordial ingredients of our creation and it not only formed the memories of our ancestors but also continues to influence our minds and hearts today. It is the driving force, the inspiration that sets man apart from the animals and allows him to dream of becoming a God.

Bibliography

- 12th Planet, The, Zecharia Sitchin, Avon Books 1976

- Ainulindale, J.R.R. Tolkien, Harper Collins Publishers 1999

- Da Vinci Code, The, Dan Brown, Double Day 2003

- Genesis Of The Grail Kings, Laurence Gardner, Transworld Publishers Ltd. 1999

- The Hobbit, J.R.R. Tolkien, Methuen Publications 1977

- The Holy Blood And The Holy Grail, Michael Baigent, Richard Leigh, Henry Lincoln, Arrow Books 1996

- The Lord Of The Rings, J.R.R. Tolkien, Harper Collins Publishers 1999

- The Lost Treasure Of The Knights Templar, Steven Sora, Destiny Books 1999

- The Master of Speech, Shannon Dorey, Trafford Publishing 2003

- Realm Of The Ring Lords, Laurence Gardner, Fair Winds Press 2002

- Silmarillion, The, J.R.R. Tolkien, Harper Collins Publishers 1999

- Valaquenta, J.R.R. Tolkien, Harper Collins Publishers 1999

- Wars Of Gods And Men, The, Zecharia Sitchin 1985

- Iraqi archaeologists uncover ancient Sumerian 'city of graves', http://www.trussel.com/prehist/news217.htm

- Hobbit-Like Human Ancestor Found in Asia, http://news.nationalgeographic.com/news/2004/10/1027_04102 7_homo_floresiensis.html

- Gilgamesh tomb believed found, http://news.bbc.co.uk/2/hi/science/nature/ 2982891.stm

- Feds Want All-Seeing Eye in Sky, http://www.wired.com/news/politics/ 0,1283,60855,00.html?tw=wn_story_related

Notes

Introduction

Chapter 1

Personal knowledge

Chapter 2 "The Glorious Quest"

1.—Tolkien, J.R.R. *The Lord of the Rings, Book One: The Ring Sets Out.* London: HarperCollins, 1994, 79-80.
2.—Tolkien, J.R.R. The Silmarillion. London: HarperCollins, 1999, xxvii.
3.—Tolkien, J.R.R. *The Silmarillion.* London: HarperCollins, 1999,*xvi.*
4.—Tolkien, J.R.R. *The Lord of the Rings, Book Two: The Ring goes South.* London: HarperCollins, 1994, 79.
5.—Tolkien, J.R.R. *Ainulindale.* London: HarperCollins, 1979, 3.
6.—Tolkien, J.R.R. *Ainulindale.* London: HarperCollins, 1979, 3.

Chapter 3 "The Coming of the Gods"

1.—Tolkien, J.R.R. *Valaquenta.* London: HarperCollins, 1979, 16.
2.—Sitchin, Z. *The 12th Planet.* New York: Avon Books, 1976, 89.
3.—Book of Enoch 7:16. Oxford: Clareden Press, 1995.
4.—Ibid, 213
5.—Gardner, Laurence. *Genesis of the Grail Kings: The Pendragon Legacy of Adam and Eve.* London: Transworld, 1999, 33.
6.—ibid. 34
7.—ibid. 101
8.—ibid. 102
9.—ibid. 110
10.—ibid. 111
11.—ibid. 101
12.—ibid. 101
13.—ibid. 44

14.—ibid. 42

15.—Dorey, S. *The Master of Speech: Dogon Mythology Reveals Genetic Engineering in Humans.* British Columbia: Trafford, 2003, 24-25.

16.—Dorey, S. *The Master of Speech: Dogon Mythology Reveals Genetic Engineering in Humans.* British Columbia: Trafford, 2003, 24.

17.—Tolkien, J.R.R. *The Silmarillion.* London: HarperCollins, 1999, xiv.

Chapter 4 "The Coming of the Elves"

1.—Tolkien, J.R.R. *The Silmarillion.* London: HarperCollins, 1979, 45.

2.—ibid. 44.

3—ibid. 46.

4—Tolkien, J.R.R. *The Lord of the Rings, Book Two: The Ring goes South.* London: HarperCollins, 1994, 14.

5.—Tolkien, J.R.R. *The Hobbit.* Toronto: Magnum, *1977, 47.*

6.—Barkho, L. "Iraqi Archaeologists Uncover Ancient Sumerian 'city of graves.'" Octbober 30, 2000. The London Times, http://www.trussel.com/prehist/news217.html (accessed February 9, 2007).

7.—page 26—The Japan Times, October 30, 2000 http://www.trussel.com/prehist/news217.htm

8.—Dorey, S. *The Master of Speech: Dogon Mythology Reveals Genetic Engineering in Humans.* British Columbia: Trafford, 2003, 8.

9.—ibid. 25-25.

10.—ibid. 26-27.

11.—ibid 26

12.—ibid. 27

Chapter 5 "The Coming of the Dwarves"

1.—Tolkien, J.R.R. *The Lord of the Rings, Book Two: The Ring goes South.* London: HarperCollins, 1994,17.

2.—Tolkien, J.R.R. *The Silmarillion.* London: HarperCollins, 1979, 37-38.

3—Tolkien, J.R.R. *The Silmarillion.* London: HarperCollins, 1979, 37-38.

Chapter 6 "The Coming of the Hobbits"

1.—Mayell, H. "Hobbit-Like Human Ancestor Found in Asia." October 27, 2004. National Geographic News, http://news.nationalgeograhic.com/news/2004/10/1027 _041027_homo_floresiensis.html (accessed February 10, 2007).

2.—Tolkien, J.R.R. *The Lord of the Rings, Book Two: The Ring goes South.* London: HarperCollins, 1994,1.

3—Wikipedea "Hobbit (Word)" http://en.wikipedea. org/wiki/Hobbit_(folklore). (accessed February 10, 2007).

4.—ibid.

Chapter 7 "The Coming of Man"

1.—Sitchin, Z. *The 12th Planet.* New York: Avon Books, 1976, 5

2—ibid. 5

3.—ibid. 337.

4.—ibid. 348.

5.—ibid. 101

6.—ibid. 101

7.—ibid. 101

Chapter 8 "The Coming of the Kings"

1.—J.R.R. Tolkien. *The Return of the King, Book Five: The War of the Ring.* London: HarperCollins, 1994, 154.

2.—Sitchin, Z. *The 12th Planet.* New York: Avon Books, 1976, 415.

3.—ibid. 99

4.—ibid. 420

5.—ibid. 421.

6.—Sitchin, Z. *The 12th Planet.* New York: Avon Books, 1976, 416.

7.—ibid. 421.

8.—Gardner, Laurence. *Genesis of the Grail Kings: The Pendragon Legacy of Adam and Eve.* London: Transworld, 1999, 1.

9.—BBC News. "Gilgamesh Tomb Believed Found." April 29, 2003. http:// news.bbc.co.uk/2/hi/science/nature/2982891.stm (accessed February 10, 2007).

10.—Sitchin, Z. *The 12th Planet.* New York: Avon Books, 1976, 422.

Chapter 9 "King Arthur and Glastonbury"

Personal knowledge

Chapter 10 "One Ring to Rule Them All"

1.—Tolkien, J.R.R. *The Fellowship of the Ring, Book One: The Ring Sets Out.* London: HarperCollins, 1994, 66.

2—Weldon, B., Wilcox, J. "The Defenders of the Ring up in Arms at Myth in the Making. August 3, 2001. http.//www.theoneroing.net/perl/newsroom/8/996862857 (accessed February 19, 2007).

3—"The Story of the Volsungs" The Online Medieval & Classical Dictionary. May 1997 http://omacl/volsunga/(accessed February 11, 2007).

Chapter 11 "The Eye of Power"

1—Tolkien, J.R.R. *The Fellowship of the Ring, Book Two: The Ring Goes South.* London: HarperCollins, 1994, 192.

2.—ibid. 196.

3.—Tolkien, J.R.R. *The Return of the King, Book Six: The End of the Third Age.* London HarperCollins, 1994, 65.

4.—Tolkien, J.R.R. *The Two Towers, Book Four: The Ring Goes West.* London, HarperCollins, 1994, 42.

5.—Dorey, S. *The Master of Speech: Dogon Mythology Reveals Genetic Engineering in Humans.* British Columbia: Trafford, 2003, 11.

6.—Sitchin, Z. *The 12th Planet.* New York: Avon Books, 1976, 307.

7.—Sitchin, Z. *The Wars of Gods and Men.* New York: Avon Books, 1985, 88.

8.—ibid. 124

9.—ibid. 296.

10.—Sora, S. *The Lost Treasure of the Knights Templar: Solving the Oak Island Mystery.* Vermont: Destiny, 1999, 228.

11.—Shachtman, N. "Feds Want All-Seeing Eye in Sky." Wired. October 17,2003. Http;//www.wired.com/news/politics/0,1283,60855,00.html

12.—ibid.

Chapter 12 "The First Battle of Gods and Men"

1.—Tolkien, J.R.R. *The Return of the King, Book Five: The War of the Ring.* London, HarperCollins, 1994, 178

2.—ibid. 179

3.—ibid. 194

4.—Sitchin, Z. *The Wars of Gods and Men.* New York: Avon Books, 1985, 26.

5.—ibid. 27

6.—ibid 28

7.—ibid 28

8.—ibid. 28

9.—ibid. 29

10.—ibid. 30

11.—ibid. 30
12.—ibid. 32
13.—ibid. 33

Chapter 13 "The Real Battle of Troy"

1.—Sitchin, Z. *The Wars of Gods and Men.* New York: Avon Books, 1985, 4.
2.—ibid. 3
3.—ibid. 4
4.—ibid. 3
5.—ibid 2
6.—ibid. 3
7.—ibid 2

Chapter 14 "The God King Called The Stormer"

1.—Tolkien. J.R.R. *The Return of the King, Book Five: The War of the Ring.* London, HarperCollins, 1994, 177.
2.—Sitchin, Z. *The 12ᵗʰ Planet.* New York: Avon Books, 1976, 134.
3.—Sitchin, Z. *The Wars of Gods and Men.* New York: Avon Books, 1985, 70.

Chapter 15—"The Truth Behind the Destruction of the Earth"

1.—Genesis 6:4 The New King James Version
2.—Genesis 6:7
3.—ibid. Genesis 7:1-4
4.—ibid. Genesis 3:7
5.—page 10
6.—Sitchin, Z. *The 12ᵗʰ Planet.* New York: Avon Books, 1976, 377.
7.—ibid. 381
8.—ibid. 101
9.—Gardner, L. *Genesis of the grail Kings."* London: Transworld, 1999, p. 72.
10.—Dorey, S. *The Master of Speech: Dogon Mythology Reveals Genetic Engineering in Humans.* British Columbia: Trafford, 2003, 37.
11.—ibid. 48.
12.—ibid. 245.
13.—ibid. 244.

Chapter 16—"Viracocha—After the Deluge"

1.—Hancock, G. *Fingerprints of the Gods: A Quest for the Beginning and the End.* London: Arrow Books, 1998, 57.

Chapter 17—"The Untold Story of Gilgamesh

1—http://news.bbc.co.uk/2/hi/science/nature/2982891.stm
2—http://www.mnsu.edu/emuseum/information/biography/klmno/layard_austen_henry.html

Chapter 18—"Legacy of the Elf-Queens"

1—Tolkien, J.R.R. *The Silmarillion.* London: HarperCollins, 1979, 117-118.
2—Sora, S. *The Lost Treasure of the Knights Templar.* Vermont: Destiny, 199, p. 126.. 3—ibid. 170-171.
4—ibid. 171.
5.—ibid. 218
6—Brown, D. *The Da Vinci Code.* New York: Anchor Books, 2003,1.

Chapter 19—"Donation of Constantine"

1.—Tolkien, J.R.R. *The Return of the King, Book Six: The End of the Third Age..* London: HarperCollins, 1994, 99.

Chapter 20—"Of Dragons and Eagles"

1.—Tolkien, J.R.R. *The Hobbit* Toronto: Metheun, 1977, 203.
2.—Warner Brothers. *Excalibur* [Motion Picture]. (1981) United Sates: Warner Brothers HomeVideo.
3.—Hogarth, P. *Dragons.* Toronto: Penguin, 1980, 13-14.
4.—Barrow, M. "The Legend of Saint George and the Dragon." Woodland's Junior School. http://woodlands-junior.kent.sch.uk/customs/stgeorge2.html/ (date accessed February 13, 2007)
5.—Hogarth, P. *Dragons.* Toronto: Penguin, 1980, 110.
6.—ibid. 151.
7.—Kren, E., Marx, D. "Pope St. Sylvester's Miracle." http://kepar.demasz.hu/arth/html/m/maso/sylveste.htm (accessed February 11, 2007)
8.—Hogarth, P. *Dragons.* Toronto: Penguin, 1980, 125.
9—Whiting, B.J. et. al., *College Survey of English Literature.* New York: Harcourt, Brace & World, 1942, 55.

10.—Hogarth, P. *Dragons.* Toronto: Penguin, 1980, 15-16.

11.—The Epoch Times "Dragon in the Tibet Sky." http://en.epochtimes.com/news/5-8-7/310303.html

12. ibid.

List of Illustrations and Photos

All of the photographs appearing in this book are owned by the author.

Through special arrangements and with great gratitude many of the illustrations appearing in this book have been kindly provided by Mary Alice Bennett of MJA Studio, Tucson, Arizona and by Heidi Murphy.

978-0-595-44093-1
0-595-44093-2